'Coriolanus' in Europe

'Coriolanus' in Europe

DAVID DANIELL

LONDON
THE ATHLONE PRESS · 1980

First published 1980 by The Athlone Press
at 90–91 Great Russell Street, London WC1B 3PY
The Athlone Press is an imprint
of Bemrose UK Limited

Distributor in U.S.A. and Canada
Humanities Press Inc, New Jersey

British Library Cataloguing in Publication Data
Daniell, David
'Coriolanus' in Europe.
1. Shakespeare, William. Coriolanus
2. Shakespeare, William – Stage history – Europe – 1950
3. Royal Shakespeare Company
I. Title
792.9   PR2805

ISBN 0 485 11192 6

Printed in Great Britain
by W & J Mackay Limited, Chatham

To the 'Coriolanus' company, and to Dorothy

'He told her also how he had been a momentary ornament of a troupe of strolling actors, engaged in the arduous task of interpreting Shakespeare to French and German . . . audiences.'

(Henry James)

Contents

Acknowledgements

It is a particular pleasure to record my thanks to many people. First, to Terry Hands, Alan Howard and the whole company, for those repeated performances of *Coriolanus*, often achieved under unusual strains and difficulties, but always with a standard of absolute excellence aimed at and attained. Next, to friends in many theatres and cities in Europe for special kindness and help: to Balbine Huet of the Théâtre National de l'Odéon, Paris; Professor Henri Fluchère; Dr Erika Zabrsa of the Burgtheater, Vienna; Danielle de Boeck of the Théâtre National, Brussels, and Ros Falvey of the British Council there; Dr Gerhard Blasche and Margaret Mieruch of the Thalia-Theater, Hamburg; Dr Michael Kerwer and Rosemarie Koch of the Schiller-Theater, West Berlin, and Hilary Bartlett of the British Council there; Gisela Schloesser of the Berliner Ensemble, East Berlin; Jorg-Dieter Haas of the Bayerisches Staatsschauspiel, Munich, and Ilse Bartlett of the British Council there. Special thanks go to Major W. G. Norman, Army Public Relations, and Cpl Philip Langan, Intelligence Corps, and to Reinhard Stegen of the Hochschule für Fernsehen und Film, Munich, for photographs in Berlin and Munich: and to Claire Scollar of Cologne and Herta Renk of Eichstätt. Among the company, abroad, I happily acknowledge many valuable conversations: with Terry Hands, Alan Howard, Graham Crowden, Maxine Audley, Jill Baker, Oliver Ford-Davies, John Burgess, Charles Dance, Bernard Brown, Barrie Rutter, Pat Connell and Nigel Garvey, and on the technical and administrative side with Bill Wilkinson, Hal Rogers, Alistair Minnigin, Brian Harris, Lucy Coghlan and most especially Philip Hoare and John Moore: the patience and kindness of these people in answering my questions, sometimes in the strangest places when they were in the middle of doing half-a-dozen other things, must go on record. My absolute indebtedness, however, is to Diane Rogers (West), Deputy Stage Manager. Without her extraordinary skills there would probably have been, each evening, no show: without her constant information, attention to detail, advice, support, friendship and general help to me, at every stage from the first day in Paris to the final submission of typescript to the printers, there would certainly have been no book.

In England, I have been greatly helped by the professional skills of Ann Strutt of Hemel Hempstead Library; of Kitsa Caswell, and most especially Doris Lord and Jacquie Brown, all of University College London. Help in translation has come from my wife, Dorothy; from Dr Rosemary Ashton of the English Department, University College; and above all from Irene Dänzer-Vanotti of Freiburg, without whose careful work at my side through over one thousand five hundred lengthy German hand-written answers to my questionnaires and other material I should have been completely lost. Nicholas Dyson has been a patient and wise editor. For special help with research it is a pleasure to thank here my younger son, Andy: for permission to use extracts from their journals Graham Crowden, Paul Basson and Stephen Humphries. I gratefully acknowledge the permission of the Governors of the Royal Shakespeare Theatre, Stratford-upon-Avon for reproduction of pages from the prompt-book: as well as Ian McKay for reproduction of his fight-plot, and Reg Wilson for his magnificent photographs of the play in performance. It is also pleasant to record my thanks to the Joint Heads of the Department of English at University College London, Professors Karl Miller and Randolph Quirk, for ten days' leave of absence to enable me to complete the tour; to the Dean of the Faculty of Arts of University College for financial assistance from the Travel Fund; and to the Central Research Funds Committee, University of London, for a grant.

My greatest debt as always is to my wife and family, who kindly supported, and even encouraged, my disappearance into yet another strange adventure.

Leverstock Green
1979

Introduction

The Royal Shakespeare Theatre at Stratford-upon-Avon enjoys its centenaries, and seems to have one every other year. Ever since David Garrick first held a Shakespeare Festival at Stratford, a waterlogged affair in tents by the Avon in 1769, all the steps to the present remarkable theatre organisation have been taken separately, so that there are a lot of milestones to remember. In 1979, the centenary was that of the opening of the first Shakespeare Memorial Theatre in Stratford.

The RSC now plays to more than a million people a year in Britain, and has a strong following abroad. Since 1960 it has won over eighty national and international awards; more, they point out in modest small print in their programmes, than any other company. As part of the 1979 celebrations, a European tour was arranged for one of the most successful productions of that season, Terry Hands' *Coriolanus* with Alan Howard in the title rôle. It was a production which showed the RSC at its best: a strong ensemble, well able to balance an international star; a dedication to the clarity of a full Shakespearean text, finely spoken; a rapidly-moving uncluttered staging which allowed scene to overlap scene and keep the dramatic phrasing; an intelligent and knowledgeable direction aiming all the time to bring out the multiple possibilities of meaning in a high Shakespearean tragedy. Bernard Levin, in *The Times*, called it 'the strongest, clearest and most consistent Shakespeare I have seen anywhere for years'.

Written in about 1608, the last of Shakespeare's great tragedies, *Coriolanus* has never been so popular as the Elizabethan *Hamlet*, nor the Jacobean *Othello*, *King Lear*, *Macbeth* or *Antony and Cleopatra* which apparently preceded it. Even so, it has not been out of mind for very long, probably since it was written, though some of the attention it has attracted has not been helpful. Some critical prejudices against the play began to change between the wars, when the taut, sinewy language of Shakespeare's later style, with little apparent lyricism but great potential of meaning below a complex, difficult surface, came more into fashion. The politics of this play, too, recently seemed more relevant. The history of the patrician Roman warrior banished by his own people, who fear his tyranny, and his joining the enemy to seek revenge, is nevertheless a story deep in European consciousness. From its apparent origins in Livy and in Plutarch's *Lives* in the first century

Volumnia (Maxine Audley), Caius Martius Coriolanus (Alan Howard) and
Menenius Agrippa (Graham Crowden).

AD have come many versions, both before and after Shakespeare, many in
French, though Shakespeare's seems to have been the first play. It has been much
adapted. In the twentieth century free alterations have been used as propaganda
by both political wings, particularly in France and Germany. It has a mildly
sensational history of being banned.

Terry Hands' production, the third RSC *Coriolanus* in a dozen years, was seen
first in Stratford in October 1977. It grew in a sense out of the very successful work
with designer Abdel Farrah, Alan Howard, and the team of actors and technicians
which, remaining largely the same, presented the two *Parts* of *Henry 4*, *Henry 5*
and the three *Parts* of *Henry 6* from 1975 on. Alan Howard was interested in the
rôle of Coriolanus: just after the interval in *Henry 6 Part Three*, Howard, playing
the old king in his Scottish captivity, came down-stage reading a little blue-
backed missal: this was in fact each night his copy of *Coriolanus*. The production
opened to very favourable notices indeed: it went the following Spring, 1978, to
Newcastle-upon-Tyne, before the first of two London seasons. Now it was going
round an already alerted Europe: a week in Paris, two days in Vienna, and then in

rapid succession time in Amsterdam, Brussels, Hamburg, Berlin, Munich and Zürich.

This touring company was not in any sense a 'touring company', specially put together for Europe. With only minor exceptions, it was the company which finished at Stratford and went on to Newcastle and London. It was certainly not a 'touring version' either. It was given at full normal length, even though this was a good hour longer than most French and German audiences can usually take their Shakespeare, even in their own languages. It had a virtually uncut text. Farrah's remarkable set, with enormous walls which slowly move so dramatically, was carried around Europe without visible modification. The ten musicians, the wind and percussion band perched on gantries high on either side of the stage playing Ian Kellam's fine music, performed throughout Europe. Terry Hands was his own lighting-designer for the production, and the complex lighting, so striking in its fluidity, so impressive on usually under-lit European stages, was unmodified. The stage-crew who travelled with the company had all worked the show through most of its English performances. The whole 'circus' (my word) was large, lively – and unexpectedly young: the technicians were looked at with some suspicion by their European local equivalents, who were usually twice their age and more, and wearing sober overalls. Those attitudes lasted only as long as it took for the RSC

The basic set in one position. The four big walls move like doors. The gantries on either side for musicians and follow-spots can just be seen.

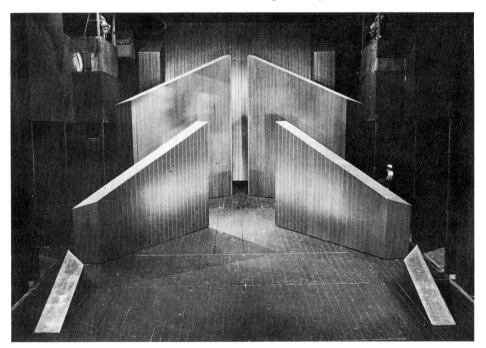

people to get to work. The full back-stage complement of the RSC caused wonder everywhere, not only at how good they were at their jobs, but at how *few* they were. Heavily state-subsidised theatres, in Austria and Germany in particular, can have as many as a dozen men to our one – and more than one of our men was a girl, anyway, which was even more unnerving.

Note: Even while this tour, so triumphant throughout Europe, was in progress, decisions were being made by the new British Government which mean that the Royal Shakespeare Company is, as this book goes to press, alarmingly threatened. The tour, which did so much for Britain's image in Europe, was modest in cost. With more money, some things could have been better: for example, the publicity, for which there was virtually no money available at all, could have spread the sound of the British success far wider.

Yet now, as I add this note a few months later, the RSC is facing permanent damage. The combination of unchecked inflation, punitive VAT on tickets, and the cuts imposed on the Arts Council grant, is already deadly. Plans for one theatre have had to be abandoned. A grant-aided body, like the RSC, has no resources of capital, and is always living close to subsistence-level. Commercial sponsorship, though apparently attractive, is no way for primary funding of the arts in Britain. The later crippling of this Company, one of Britain's richest national assets, is the ironic, tragic, footnote to this book.

One

Paris I

Théâtre National de l'Odéon, Paris. Tuesday morning 3 April. My first experience of a working theatre, and disconcerting. No-one had told me that it would be pitch dark. To get back-stage I go down steps, into what seems absolute blackness. I can hear people at work close by, some talking harsh Parisian French. I wait to let my eyes get accustomed, and move cautiously forward and round, and step on to the wall-enclosed stage into not much more light. There are a lot of people, most of them young. A cheerful, busy girl in an RSC sweat-shirt and jeans smiles – I recognise her as someone who checked names on the coach from Charles de Gaulle airport last night. Feeling naïve and alien, I ask her why it is so dark. She introduces herself: Diane West, she says, DSM. She tells me that they are focussing. I try to look wise, and glance to the top of the steel tower on the sloping stage, where a young man is adjusting a lamp. She explains that DSM means Deputy Stage Manager, and that she sits beside the stage with the prompt-copy during a performance and gives all the cues. I suddenly look at her intelligently – I remember Terry Hands speaking of her, and doing so with deep respect.

I go and sit in the stalls out of the way, and watch. It is instantly obvious that some process I have never imagined is taking place. A lot of people are doing a lot of different things at the same time in the same small place, without at all getting in each other's way. How this trick is worked is a mystery. Moreover, lights come and go, but no-one stops what he is doing because it is suddenly dark. Half the people on stage are speaking French, and half are speaking English, and no-one seems even to notice. The house-lights come up suddenly, and I find that the theatre I am sitting in is very pretty. Down a little passage near me, Diane West is explaining to two follow-spot operators *'Pour effet six, C'est très important pour . . .* avoid . . . what's avoid? . . . *éviter les yeux . . .'* A smooth French voice takes over . . . *'attention éviter les yeux des acteurs'.*

On the coach from the Aldwych to Heathrow, Hal Rogers, the Tour Manager, had explained to me that every year touring abroad became more and more complicated. Not only were shows themselves technically more complex to mount: more performances had to be fitted in to every trip, because costs were rising so fast that more effort had to be made to recoup. One result of this could be too little time

Leaving the Aldwych at the start of the tour. Left to right, Graham Crowden, Richard Derrington, Charles Dance, Stephen Jenn, Bille Brown.

between performances in different cities. For example, leaving Paris and getting in to Vienna in ten days' time would be critical. The journey by road should take the lorries twenty-nine hours, and they should arrive in Vienna at noon the day before the RSC first night there. Yet even if the lorries left Paris on time, and crossed all the frontiers without delay, the pressures to get the show opening on time in Vienna were going to be intense.

The company's arrival in Paris was not good. The flight from Heathrow was delayed by seven hours. At midnight, driving slowly through the narrow streets to the hotels, people's tempers were understandably short. Many of this fine company started their foreign tour distinctly miserable.

Tuesday afternoon. Philip Hoare, the unflappable Stage Manager, has just announced, from the stage, 'We're going to run through all the battle-cues.' I stand in the wings, tucked into a corner by a large sound control-board, hoping I'm invisible. In front of me John Moore, kneeling and wearing headphones, looks large and comfortable. There is a faint smell of soldering-resin on a hot iron, and a bench littered with tools and meters and plugs and wire. John, an obvious boffin, gazes at two wires as if he has never seen them before, and with an air of experiment joins them together. He knows precisely what he is doing, of course, and is widely admired in theatrical-sound circles.

Behind John it is very dark. There is a gleam of helmets, a faint flash of spears amid the black drapes. The scaffolding, the masking and the cables make spear-holding hazardous. On stage, the big walls are slowly pulled and pushed with cheerful French cries and a few, low-voiced patient words from Alistair Minnigin and Neil Robson, Chief Stage Technicians. For the local staff, synchronising the movements, getting them exact, and staying out of sight, take a little practice.

Alan Howard, in working clothes but wearing his studded gloves, jumps hard on to the stage to test it. He wants a complete run-through of act one when the battle-sequences have been tried.

A sudden huge noise of drums and full brass from the gantry over my head doesn't quite drown the calls, some of them very urgent, for light here and there. Ian Kellam's magnificent full Roman war-music accompanies the constant battle to get the lighting ready, plotted cue by cue (there are over a hundred) for the French electricians. This lighting-plotting is slow and I sense a source of tension.

There is heavy sawing and banging near me, as the under-spoken, muttered run-through goes on. Some-one shouts 'One, two, three, go!', and again a quiet voice says 'Let's try again, shall we . . . Once more, we get to here . . .' Roman soldiers practice running on, and off, at great speed, together, without getting spears tangled in the cables. A shout, 'Check which number it is, Philip, will yer? Fifteen is it?' Philip calls, 'It's forty-nine.'

Caius Martius (Alan Howard), Titus Lartius (Roy Purcell) and the victorious Roman army.

He goes unhurriedly off-stage to an illuminated alcove, like an aumbry in an ancient church, which holds a copy of The Book, a small lamp, and a microphone. His quietly pastoral voice goes out over the back-stage tannoy 'Company on stage, please. Scene fourteen. Scene fourteen on stage, please.'

I go into the stalls. I learn that what I am watching is 'a Technical', that is, a rehearsal with words hardly audible, to get the technicalities of everything else right. A board across some seats in the centre of the stalls has on it a reading-light, a mass of papers and a mike. At this Production Desk sits a young man of distinctly scruffy appearance, his long hair in tight ropes: a bright, attractive red-head called Jacqui, who is interpreting for the young man, speaking into the mike, which squawks back at them in curt French, and Di, who seems to be everywhere. The young man, who looks like someone in a Fifth Form any Headmaster would persuade to leave, is spoken of with awe, and is apparently called Basher, simply. He is a Lighting Designer for the RSC: his name, which nobody uses, is Brian Harris, and he seems to do without sleep or food.

In England, the complications of preparing the set in its various sections, and getting it loaded on to the lorries for the cross-channel ferry on the previous Thursday evening, had been increased by three factors. Some of the set, like the moving walls and the huge side-gantries on which the musicians sat, was at the Aldwych, where it had been in use until the previous Saturday night. Other things were at Stratford, whence they had to travel in the specially packed container. A new set-floor with all its underlying mass of raked rostra gates, was being built – or rather adapted from another set – by a specialist scenery-builder in East London, round the clock, without time to fit it up and test it, or fit many trimmings, before it all had to be loaded into the two containers. The order of packing was vital, of course, because getting quickly off the lorries into the theatres depended on it. Final complications of actually finishing the building, then loading the containers on to the big transporter-lorries, where they would live for six weeks, getting the RSC logos on the sides, checking lists of everything, including props, costumes, musical instruments, and general paraphernalia, was all done in about forty-eight hours. Though Philip Hoare had three weeks before made the lists, seen that props and wardrobe lists and follow-spot plots were being translated and sent on, and organised movements, a bottle-neck at Stratford caused great haste at the end. An absolute deadline for finally locking the vans was in fact overshot by ten minutes. Indeed one of the vertical ladders for the musicians to use on the gantries was made, it seems, in about three minutes. Philip Hoare explained: 'Everybody was working. I was working with a great screwdriver, the driver of the lorry was planing, a man from the drawing-office was down with a drill in one hand and a phone in the other, . . . there were six of us on that ladder, which was supposed to have treads rather than rungs, but we hadn't time . . . someone was going along with a drill, someone was whopping

The set-floor being assembled on stage.

glue on, someone was putting screws in, I was screwing them in, the driver was planing off the edges, and then we threw it on the van.'

Arrangements at Calais had then gone wrong. The two lorries should have cleared customs there, as Hal Rogers had arranged. That couldn't be done, so they were sent to Paris, to the Gare du Nord. There the drivers were told no, they had to go to Versailles. By the time the drivers got to Versailles it was half past four on Friday, with not a customs man in sight. They were told by the French authorities to go back during office hours on Monday morning. Philip Hoare explained again: 'But unless the lorries had started unloading at eight sharp on Monday morning at the Odéon, the show would never open on Tuesday. So we just got on and unloaded, without customs clearance at all. Because of this, we are now in difficulties at the other end, at the get-out from the Odéon into the lorries. We estimate that they should be on the road to Vienna by four in the morning at the very latest. But the customs people are saying that we have to report to Versailles at nine-thirty that morning for the lorries to be checked and the carnets stamped.'

What Hal Rogers had said about complications and speed was becoming strikingly illustrated. Of course speed is endemic to this kind of theatre: most things are done at the last minute. In initial rehearsal periods, decisions about costumes or set are left as late as possible. In that phrase 'as late as possible', what 'possible' means often looks, from outside, starkly impossible. The movements of Terry Hands, for example, over the period in which *Coriolanus* finished in Paris and ran in Vienna make that very clear: he spent half of each of four days with us,

The RSC lorries at the back of the Burgtheater, Vienna.

in Paris or Vienna, and half at Covent Garden. His *Coriolanus* in Vienna and *Parsifal* in London opened simultaneously, and he was, in effect, present at both. Another kind of 'impossible' had been in the schedule of Terry Murphy, the specialist scenery-builder in London. As Philip Hoare said, 'We don't build scenery any more so much as have tremendous construction-sites . . . its an engineering job . . . the back wall alone for *Coriolanus* in the original set weighed more than a ton.' Any decision-chain is long: whether an overseas tour is actually going to happen or not may depend not only on whether the principal actors are free, and willing, and have finally made up their minds to go, but also on the movements of distant governments. So work at the end will often have to be done at speed. To meet the deadline Terry Murphy and his crew worked for fifty-three hours without stopping.

Another clear 'impossible' was Terry Hands' lighting. The RSC took with them thirty of the famous new little twenty-four volt 'mini-beams', so effective in his *Henry 6* and *The Changeling* productions, and other lamps, including five big follow-spots. The rest depended on local resources. Though follow-spot plot-sheets had been sent on ahead, the work of positioning and focussing lamps, fixing and recording all the light-levels for dozens of lamps on over a hundred different cues on eight different lighting-boards with varying sophistication (to say nothing of varying voltages), rehearsing local follow-spot operators, and arranging cues in French or German or Flemish or Dutch, would all have to be done from scratch in each place in a day – and that assumed that the 'electrics', the men who did the work, were quick on the up-take in every theatre.

It is moreover a difficult play to get right, with not a shred of relief from the relentless concentration on the central figure. Whether he is present or not, nobody talks about anything else through the entire play but the man Coriolanus. There is no Clown, no Ghost, nor even a visible villain. Though adaptors and translators twist and bend the material, as Shakespeare wrote the play it is impossible to point a finger and say unequivocally 'hero, to be admired' or 'villian, to be hissed'. In spite of a certain starkness of language, ambiguity, ambivalence, is everywhere. It tends to be hard to play, and to watch. It has frequently been loaded with irrelevances, from political meanings to visible 'singing tradesmen', but Terry Hands' production insisted on three and a half hours of the closest attention to one figure who sets out not to be liked. Schedule, set, lighting and even the drama itself were all 'impossible'.

During a performance or rehearsal, Di as DSM normally sat at a desk at the side of the stage, so that she could see a good deal of the stage, with, open in front of her, the prompt copy. This massive interleaved script contains not only, of course, the text, from which a prompt would be given if one were called for, but a record of all stage-movements, and all the cues – for every change of light or set, for all entries and music; and a check-list of properties for each scene. This prompt copy, being one kind of record of part of a company's work, is particularly valuable, a tradition going back at least to Shakespeare's time. John Moore had built for the RSC a cue-board, a rectangular box with rows of keys and lights, from which the network of red and green cue-lights to every point around the stage could be controlled. So Di normally sat with her fingers at the keys, looking at the book, glancing at the stage.

The control of stage-lighting varies in sophistication from theatre to theatre. The RSC's theatre at Stratford has the most up-to-date system in the world, a 'memory board' which makes the plotting, correcting and operating of lighting, however complex, very efficient and fast. Elsewhere, one might find, say, something as old-fashioned as a punched-card controlled board; or even something really primitive, as at the Odéon, where the lighting changes were worked by operators standing at a wall of ranks of dimmer-switches worked by big levers, moving everything laboriously by hand. There, however skilful, willing and good-natured the operators are – and those at the Odéon were certainly all three – making a lighting plot is exceedingly slow. The process had been further held up that day because the RSC had been given, or at least had retransmitted, wrong information about voltages. As the first day went by, the lighting-plot was progressing with horrifying slowness. As the time approached for the first performance, Basher and the Odéon electricians were still writing the lighting-plot for the middle act, with the long last act still to do as well.

Five minutes before the show started, Di was told that the 'electrics', the lighting operators, needed verbal cues as well as light-signals. She had already

⑦⑥

n.b. Aed. dressed as Volscian soldier.

| 1st.Vol. | 2nd.Vol | 3rd.V.sen | 2nd.V.sen | Lieut | AED |

LX 20 (INST) ↑⁴/s   LX 21 (INST) ↓⁴/s
F/S B OUT   ↓ᵈ/s   F/S D , E   ↑ᵈ/s

✕   1ST. LOCK
         Aed. + Lieut. rise into Lock
⁴/s breach line

_____

BREAK
| 1st.V. | 2nd.V | 1st.V.sen | Lieut | Aed | (2nd Vol. sen ex.ᶜˡ) |

✕   2ND. LOCK
         1V 2V 1st.V Lieut AED
              sen
         2R   SR MAR 1R   7R
                    ↑
                    /
                    /

LX 22   (3ᵉ) ↑ ⁴/s ↓ ᵈ/s
LX 23   (3ᵉ) F/S A,D,E OUT   ↓⁴/s ↑ᵈ/s

WALL Q4   ⁴/s PS Wall to on/off posit.ⁿ
           ⁴/s OP   " follows
           Mart. onto walls
           F/O — ⁴/s WALLS OPEN ᴰ/s

TO   RED/BLUE

        F/o

TO   YELLOW

───────────────────────────────

①
⌐2¬   ⌐7¬
⌐5¬   ⌐1⌐
⌐4¬
MAR ←   TL

Vols. form line ⁴/s
on ⁴/s breach line - Lieut + Aed. kneel

② Roms. regroup facing ⁴/s —

| MART | 2ⁿᵈ | 4ᵗʰ | 5ᵗʰ | 1st | 7ᵗʰ | TL |

③ Roms ✕ ⁴/s into Lock with Vol.
   ↑ Mart. ✕ to Lock — adds own sword.
   Break lock — exit ᶜ/R 4ᵗʰR.
                      ᶜ/L TL , 2nd V.sen

   Roms ✕ ᵈ/s , crouch, lie —
   Mart. ✕ C   2 5   1   7

④ Roms. rise, regroup —

        ⌐5¬
   ⌐2¬   MAR ⌐1¬

⑤ Roms ✕ ⁴/s into Lock with Vol.
   Vols — 1st V   2nd V   4th V.sen   Lieut   Aed.

   Roms— ⌐2¬ ⌐5¬   MAR   ⌐1⌐   ⌐7¬
           PD   DSP   BR   IM

   Break lock — exit ᶜ/R 1st. Vol.sen.
                      ᵈ/R 3rd. Vol.sold.
   Roms ✕ ᵈ/s , relax.

        2   MART   7
            5   1

⑥ Roms rise   2 5   1   7
   2nd Vol.sold & Lieut exit ᵘ/c thro' gates
   Mart. ✕ ⁴/s , thro' gates
   Rom solds ✕ ⁴/s to gates, as gates close,
       hold up spears across gates /
   Rom solds. break ᵈ/s.

Two pages of the prompt copy.

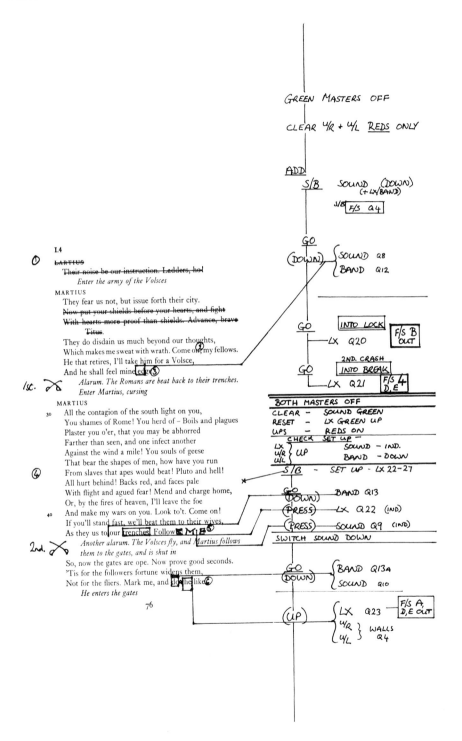

I.4

① ~~LARTIUS~~
~~Their noise be our instruction. Ladders, ho!~~
Enter the army of the Volsces
MARTIUS
They fear us not, but issue forth their city.
~~Now put your shields before your hearts, and fight~~
~~With hearts more proof than shields. Advance, brave~~
~~Titus.~~
They do disdain us much beyond our thoughts,
Which makes me sweat with wrath. Come on, my fellows. ②
He that retires, I'll take him for a Volsce,
And he shall feel mine edge ③

1sc.   *Alarum. The Romans are beat back to their trenches.*
Enter Martius, cursing
MARTIUS
30   All the contagion of the south light on you,
You shames of Rome! You herd of – Boils and plagues
Plaster you o'er, that you may be abhorred
Farther than seen, and one infect another
Against the wind a mile! You souls of geese
That bear the shapes of men, how have you run
④   From slaves that apes would beat! Pluto and hell!
All hurt behind! Backs red, and faces pale
With flight and agued fear! Mend and charge home,
Or, by the fires of heaven, I'll leave the foe
40   And make my wars on you. Look to't. Come on!
If you'll stand fast, we'll beat them to their wives,
As they us to our trenches. Follow M B ⑤

2nd.   *Another alarum. The Volsces fly, and Martius follows*
them to the gates, and is shut in
So, now the gates are ope. Now prove good seconds.
'Tis for the followers fortune widens them,
Not for the fliers. Mark me, and do the like ⑥
He enters the gates
76

GREEN MASTERS OFF

CLEAR 4/R + 4/L REDS ONLY

ADD
S/B   SOUND (DOWN)
              (+ LX/BAND)
S/B F/S Q4

GO
(DOWN)   SOUND Q8
         BAND Q12

GO   INTO LOCK   F/S B
— LX Q20   OUT

         2ND. CRASH
GO   INTO BREAK   F/S
— LX Q21   D,E 4

BOTH MASTERS OFF
CLEAR – SOUND GREEN
RESET – LX GREEN UP
UPS   – REDS ON
     CHECK SET UP –
LX
4/R } UP   SOUND – IND.
4/L   BAND – DOWN
S/B – SET UP – LX 22-27
GO
(DOWN)   BAND Q13
(PRESS) LX Q22 (IND)
(PRESS) SOUND Q9 (IND)
SWITCH SOUND DOWN

GO
(DOWN)   BAND Q13A
         SOUND Q10

(UP)   LX Q23 — F/S A,
                  D,E OUT
         4/R } WALLS
         4/L   Q4

The DSM, Diane West, with prompt-copy, cue-board and microphone.

arranged to cue the four follow-spot operators verbally over their headsets in French and English. Now, with minutes to go, she was given another, separate mike, for the main lighting-cues. So in addition to following the prompt-book, and working the cue-board, she was going to have to give bilingual cues over one mike, and wholly French cues over another mike – and at the same time, and under stress, not forget the French for a number like ninety-eight when she hadn't spoken French for years . . . It was, of course, 'impossible'. But she Vaselined her lips, sent for a glass of water, took a deep breath, and began.

I had never seen the start of a show from backstage before. There had been a sharp rise in adrenalin-flow at the afternoon's run-through: at night, there was a difference in kind as well as degree. Actors one would chat to on the street, or smile at waiting for rehearsal, now had a quite new quality in all the backstage area; more than concentration, something intense, an electric field, a radio-activity, something wholly unapproachable.

Normally in this production there was a first, short interval between act one and act two. On this first night in Paris that interval was stretched to over twenty minutes, to give Basher and the electricians a chance to get on with the lighting-plot for the later act. The house-lights were only half up, to discourage people from leaving – it was said there would be difficulty in getting them back from the bar. So the audience for that first night in Paris were treated a little strangely. They were themselves in places a little odd. Several in the front rows slept fitfully – it was hot, and not everybody on a continental first night, as we discovered, is a theatre-lover. A woman in the middle of the front row had a large powerful torch with which she read the play, throughout, only varying her head-down position to shift a little in her seat, when she shone the torch straight up on to the dark stage. ('It might even help' said Philip, watching her do that, 'knowing the state of the lighting . . .')

From Graham Crowden's Journal, Tuesday 3 April. The show went up at eight. Lighting not quite right, but improvisation here and there good – it was always bright enough. Went quite well. Everyone a little tense just in case walls and lights and music didn't coincide correctly. The play overran of course. Five to twelve before last calls were taken. Cheers and applause.

That first night's performance got cheers and that regular rhythmic clap with which a French house shows its appreciation, but it was all a shade respectful rather than rapturous. Backstage there were some strong feelings about the general state of unreadiness with which it was felt the show had had to go on. The involvement of the French stage-crews, however, was much appreciated: they clearly cared deeply about it as a show, with true theatrical spirit, which was not the case, it was later found, throughout Europe.

   After the first performance there was a reception for all the RSC party, given by the Odéon, a pleasant affair in the grand upstairs foyer. The Odéon staff were young and enthusiastic and cheerful, and the occasion was informal. The official reception for us, with all the diplomatic and cultural luminaries of Paris, had been held without us the night before – it had finished before we left Heathrow. An older, rather formidable, man replied to my question about whether or not the play was hard to follow by saying, with the faintest hint of a twinkle in the eye, that he had not found it hard because he had once played one of the Tribunes, Sicinius Velutus. He was, then, an actor? Yes. And now? Ah, now, Director of the Comédie Française. This was Pierre Dux himself. He had, happily, much enjoyed his evening.

Thanks to Balbine Huet, the press attaché at the Odéon – whom I heard described as the best in Europe – the Paris press had prepared for the arrival of *Coriolanus* for some time. A detailed agency message ten days before had listed the four previous RSC productions to visit Paris from 1957, and noted Alan Howard in the last two. Also listed were Terry Hands' seven previous Paris productions in seven years. *L'Express* under the bold heading 'Book your seats' gave a glowing advance notice. *Le Nouvel Observateur* advised early booking: 'Although Shakespeare may be very difficult to understand in the original language, this kind of production

Terry Hands (Director).

attracts many people . . .' and it has *'le grand acteur Alan Howard'*. *Le Figaro*'s advance notice began with a verbal snapshot of Terry Hands: 'He juggles with timetables, swallows his bacon and eggs in Vienna, his tea in London, and a glass of Beaujolais in Paris, sleeps four hours a night, one eye on a score of Wagner, one ear listening to Shakespeare. He has just finished putting on *As You Like It* at the Burgtheater in Vienna to start *Parsifal* at Covent Garden, all the time perfecting his work on *Coriolanus* . . . An intense activity, but he hardly has an dark circles under his eyes. With an air of nonchalance, his young man's figure with a mocking smile, and ironic sidelong glance, saunters through halls, airports and hotels'. An account of the play concludes, 'A tragedy in the grand Greek tradition, . . . *une symphonie fantastique sur fond de marche militaire et de Requiem'*. *L'Aurore* wrote under the heading 'An élite company, condemned to success!' quoting Hands' *'Non, ce n'est pas une pièce politique. C'est un destin individuel qui intéressait Shakespeare et nous intéresse encore.'*

A dozen articles, all but two with excellent pictures, and two of feature-length (one of fifteen hundred words) all appeared *before* the opening night: they showed a keen involvement with Shakespeare. *Les Nouvelles Littéraires*, for example, speculated on the source of Shakespeare's interest in Coriolanus – was it through Florio and Montaigne, or through the fall of Essex perhaps? Certainly the tragedy is Shakespeare's most perfect artistic success, though *'une pièce aride'* lacking *'la poésie sublime'*. The article notes how strange it is that Shakespeare chose his Roman themes from before and after but not during the Republic: perhaps there

Ian Kellam (Music).

was in that time not enough for the Renaissance interest in the individual. Yet *'Coriolanus, c'est le constat de faillite de l'humanisme. Et le héros n'a plus qu'à se réfugier dans "a world elsewhere".'*

After the first performance, the *Agence France Presse* described in a long, very enthusiastic comment the packed house, its acclaim for Howard and equally for the whole company, and how at the interval, and on the way out, one heard only unanimous praise: 'What a lesson', 'That reconciles me to the theatre', 'The English are incomparable'. Curiously hinting at politics, it points out that the Comédie Française seemed to welcome this play every twenty-three years, in 1933, in 1956, and now, adding that if it were not a fascist play then at least it is *'antidémagogique'*. 'Last night, however, it was for particularly artistic reasons that the public showed its enthusiasm to Alan Howard, who seemed to have stepped down from the pedestal of a Roman statue. He has the power, the impact of a wild beast, with impeccable diction'. There is praise for excellence right through the company.

Le Figaro had, back in August 1978, printed a long, finely-written and appreciative account of *Coriolanus* in London by Jean-Jacques Gautier, of the Académie Française, under the title *'Une victoire de Terry Hands'*, with the highest possible praise for Howard and Hands, and for the *'troupe homogène'* they work with. Now, *Figaro's* Pierre Marcabru remarked that the RSC actors use the language of tragedy, English, in a way altogether astonishing in their suppleness and freedom,

Farrah (Designer).

and their richness in changes of tone and accent. Coriolanus is not a French classical Roman: he is a young British gentleman, a bit of a snob, fragile, gallant, choleric, self-absorbed, condescending. He has received a good education '(Oxford? Cambridge?)' but he is fundamentally naïve and uncertain. His relation with his mother (*'sans freudisme trop apparent'*) is central. 'We are far from the trigger-happy, brassy fascist proposed by Franch producers'.

Playing now at the Odéon, we wondered what might happen; the common people in the play, even when spoken for by their newly-appointed Tribunes, do attract some strong invective; and Shakespeare's *Coriolanus* has had a lively political history in Paris. The Odéon is of course a sister theatre of the Comédie Française, and there, in the first weeks of 1934, this play was made the occasion for outbursts by extreme Right-wing factions in the audience. The play continued in repertory, the two or three performances a week becoming the centre of increasing agitation in and around the theatre. Fascist activity in Paris reached a climax in the violent riots of 1934 which brought down the new premier, Daladier: for a while it seemed that Parliamentary government in France might cease. Daladier, just before, had replaced the Director of the Comédie by the chief of the Sûreté. (See the note on these happenings at the end of Chapter 3.) More recently, I am told, de Gaulle objected to the play's effect: early in his period of power in 1958 he had reason to operate a censorship, it is said: under his ban apparently came Genet's *The Balcony*, and *The Screens* – and Shakespeare's *Coriolanus*. (There

is no record of such a ban in the records of the Comédie.) In the famous disturbances of May 1968 the students of Paris took possession of the Odéon theatre,
and many books and papers were burned. Ten days before we arrived at the
Odéon, there were sudden demonstrations against dismissals in the steel indus-
try which ended in violence at the Place de L'Opéra – the worst disruption in Paris
since May 1968, involving either 50,000 or 150,000 people according to which
side's figures you took. Were we now going to be the cause of more unrest in a
volatile city? *Coriolanus* had apparently, half a century before, been used to help to
spark the events which nearly destroyed the French Parliament. After our first
night it seemed that perhaps, playing an uncut text in difficult English late into the
night, all we would provoke would be sleep.

Far back-stage on Wednesday afternoon, a distant splendid music came down the
corridors of the Odéon, from the upstairs foyer. Drawn by sweet sounds like
some-one on Prospero's island, I went through and sat out of sight on the grand
staircase, and listened to the RSC Brass Quintet rehearsing. They were preparing
for the concerts they were to give on their own account as part of the RSC tour,
and the music with which they were to entertain assembling audiences wherever
possible. The larger complement of the stage-band, nine instrumentalists and a
conductor, contributed vastly to the good-humour of everyone on the tour. All
young, all cheerfully extrovert, they seemed to get the maximum out of whatever
was happening. Whether in numbing airport lounges with many hours' delay,
tramping the bitter streets in one of Europe's coldest Springs in memory, or
looking for food after the show at one in the morning, to be with the band was to
be in a cheerful area of higher spirits and wit. These were the characteristics too of
the concert-music they played: their fanfare, as well as ringing, was jovial.

That second evening, before the show, I sat for a while with Lucy Coghlan, who,
by herself, looks after Make-up and Wigs for the whole company. Two or three
actors looked after themselves entirely; most came to Lucy. As I sat, Charles
Dance, who played Aufidius, sat in leather trousers at the lighted mirror, while
the top of his body was made up. It was, I found, a silent business: not at all like a
visit to the barber's. There was a tension everywhere for the show, almost a smell
of building nervous energy. The fitting of a wig was a long and very careful
business, Lucy's young fingers touching, adjusting, re-making, in the greatest
detail. Philip's voice came over the tannoy, 'Good evening, ladies and gentlemen.
This is the half-hour call. Half an hour, please.' This meant that it was thirty-five
minutes before the start of the show – I found at first the technicalities of timing as
baffling as in a Navy – and that we were in that mystic 'Half' when the cast and
technicians and everyone are together just before the show. Di visited, notebook
in hand, to see that everything was all right. Terry suddenly appeared, smiling,
appreciative, quiet. (I was conscious that the troupe instantly relaxed because he

was there. He would, too, I knew, have a great effect on the work of re-lighting.) Ruth Rosen (Valeria), as she sat, talked a little. I was surprised by the change in appearance when a wig was fitted. I knew Ruth, and it was Ruth sitting there; but something else had happened. It was not only the wig, of course: her face was changing to match.

The quarter-hour was called. Lucy worked with hasteless speed. People came and went. Alan Howard needed twenty minutes for make-up, so she had taken him first; she knew without looking who should come where. The tannoy spoke again: 'Company, this is Hal . . .' He explained very carefully a serious problem that would arise in ten days' time, when we were trying to get back to England from Vienna. The air-traffic controllers at Heathrow had announced a go-slow for that day. Hal outlined two alternative routes to get us all back, one via Frankfurt and Gatwick, another via Paris, and, if need be, by the cross-channel ferry. He needed to know what we thought by the act two interval. I went down and stood in a thicker patch of darkness in the wings.

Two

The Play

The play began in near-darkness, with an amplified, but still soft, triple-heart-beat drum. A tight group of seven citizens moved rapidly down the raked stage, through dim light, to the front, all holding staves. One banged his staff, and in a burst of light the First Citizen (Barrie Rutter) called from the edge of the stage to the entire house, 'Before we proceed any further, hear me speak.' 'Speak,' shouted the citizens in unison, and the lines followed in urgent sentences and chorussed replies.

Shakespeare announces in that first line two of the central occupations of the play, a relationship between voice and action. Terry Hands announced the nature of his production in the discipline of unison speaking, the choreography of the close, nuclear group. The First Citizen with blazing eyes and face raised to the highest gallery urged the city to rise against Caius Martius – 'chief enemy to the people'. These citizens, in blacks, browns and greens in leather and wool, capped, jacketed and trousered, will have corn at their own price, if they succeed in killing Caius Martius. Though individual voices came through, they were a slice of a small mob, and – they heard shouts as 'the other side of the city is risen' – not the only mob in Rome.

Their rush up stage, on the way to the Capitol and intended assassination, was checked by Menenius Agrippa, patrician. Terry Hands' Rome, it was already clear, was not to be a place of social and antiquarian illustration. The audience would not watch, as Sicinius says later, the 'tradesmen singing in their shops and going/About their functions friendly'. Instead, it was a strong, black, raked acting-space with massive walls (giving, as they moved later, some scalp-raising effects) in which a fuller range of feeling than the bare set would suggest could all be defined by the inventiveness and fluidity of the lighting and music.

Graham Crowden's Menenius Agrippa (from 29 May the part was played by Paul Imbusch), over a head taller than the citizens, was – as were all the patricians – in ankle-length full-sleeved black velvet studded with silver, a great black and silver cummerbund marking his status. Capped for out-of-doors, Crowden carried a shooting stick, and with an ornate fan cooled his Tintoretto head. He here

The Citizens. Left to Right: Ron Cook, Barrie Rutter, Arthur Whybrow, David Shaw-Parker, Philip Dunbar, Iain Mitchell.

subdues the potential rioters a little and subjects their folly to a witty, acerbic analysis. He tells them his fable of the belly, arguing that the senators of Rome naturally receive the food-supply, because

> No public benefit which you receive
> But it proceeds or comes from them to you,
> And no way from yourselves.

He first presents two more of the play's devices – constant references to the human body, and a special habit of sudden hyperbole. Voice, action, body and enlargement all sound through the language of the dialogue with the First Citizen. Crowden settled himself comfortably on his shooting-stick mid-stage for his 'pretty tale' with the Citizens, grouped now less urgently, around him, relaxing one by one.

To them entered suddenly down-stage that patrician, who is himself, absolutely and surpassingly, incarnate voice and action incorporate, magnified to giant enlargement, Caius Martius. Alan Howard, bare-armed, skin-tight black leather making a silver-studded battle-dress, with a jewelled band round his brow, frightened the scattering citizens with his towering physical presence. He swung in fuller light downstage a pace or two among them, driving them like sheep together.

Shakespeare gives us a good long look at his principal, in the act (according to his own lights) of dealing with a civil riot. Howard's Caius Martius here was by no means unattractive, though imperious. Linked with him, are two more elements, a love of metaphysical opposites, and powerful fantasy:

> He that depends
> Upon your favours, swims with fins of lead,
> And hews down oaks with rushes.

Caius Martius tells Menenius of the success of the other part of the insurrection: representatives of the people – Tribunes – have been granted. He now gathers voice, action, body, hyperbole, oppositions and fantasy to a point of high invective which suddenly breaks in his response to the news that 'the Volsces are in arms'. Howard, meeting the Messenger centre-stage, arms spread, paused before his 'I . . am . . *glad* . . on't.' Immediately, on 'See, our best elders' four

The Tribunes. Sicinius Velutus (John Burgess) and Junius Brutus (Oliver Ford-Davies).

The Volscians. Tullus Aufidius (Charles Dance) with Second Volscian Senator (Stephen Jenn) and First Volscian Senator (Desmond Stokes).

Senators in full black velvet and silver, like Menenius, swept him forward, making rapid military arrangements – the Volscian leader, Tullus Aufidius, is a lion that Caius Martius is proud to hunt. Two very new Tribunes in light coats were slightly ahead of them. Caius Martius will lead one force, Cominius another, with overall command, and Titus Lartius another. The stage clears rapidly, leaving, – and thus, isolating, as so often happens in the play – only the two Tribunes, Junius Brutus and Sicinius Velutus.

Alone, these two (Oliver Ford-Davies and John Burgess) stood immobile, one clutching a leather satchel. Their new gowns of office hung a little awkwardly, worn over black Nehru-jackets, which gave them pockets, when they got used to them, to put hands in, in calculated, thoughtful gestures. They moved hardly at all, and talked carefully, surprised by events, cunning and acutely watchful. They were already established by Hands not as 'characters' in a nineteenth-century sense, but as something more like figures in a frieze.

Scene 2 (Act One, scene two)

Drums and a stereo double rattle effect accompanied the sudden strong side-lighting of a bas-relief upstage – a triptych: two black-velvet gold-studded figures in follow-spots facing inward to a central golden-headed warrior powerfully lit in powerful stance. These still figures, the Volsces, 'Tullus Aufidius *with Senators of Corioles*', spoke, in a strong echo-effect, of their preparations to meet the three Roman war-leaders and other forces. Aufidius (Charles Dance) reports to the Senators that his plans for a surprise attack on Rome have been disrupted by Roman espionage, and swears

If we and Caius Martius chance to meet,
'Tis sworn between us, we shall ever strike
Till one can do no more.

Voice and action, though in a different mode, are still dominant: this short scene is enough to establish Caius Martius' great enemy, and his ambience of spying, pretence, surprise and combat.

Scene 3 (Act One, scene three)

The soft quadraphonic triple drum-beat returned in another brief moment of darkness while a stool was placed. Downstage Caius Martius' young wife Virgilia in pale grey (Jill Baker) sat sewing. His mother Volumnia (Maxine Audley) in full black velvet stood beside her. Some dominant ideas of the play appear here in the new linking of military action and love-making. Volumnia, fantasising, looks out and 'sees' her son bloody at the wars, to the distress of the young wife. Entreated by a distinguished neighbour, Valeria, to go visiting, Virgilia will not 'over the threshold till my lord return from the wars'. Jill Baker gave the statuesque silences of Virgilia a strong erotic, private appeal. The interior setting too, is refreshing: but even in such private domesticity Shakespeare does not let go for a moment the absolute concentration of attention on one man. Valeria brings news that Cominius and his army have gone to meet the Volscian army, and that Caius Martius and Titus Lartius with their forces are set down before the city of Corioles.

Scene 4 (Act One, scene four)

Enter Martius and Titus Lartius '*with drum and colours, with Captains and Soldiers, as before the city Corioles*' as the Folio Stage-Direction has it. A great noise of tympani and short, heavy brass chords and calls made Roman music. In sudden glows of light in the darkness, the upstage walls moved inwards to form the leaves of giant gates. Roman soldiers in round, visored helmets faced their leader Caius Martius as he swung downstage with Titus Lartius. These forces are hoping to make short work of capturing Corioles, so that they can go on to assist Cominius in the main battle, against Aufidius. The Volscian army issued from the parting of the great gates before, to full brass and percussion, battle was joined upstage, Caius Martius pressing from behind. The Romans, defeated by Volscian spears, fell back downstage in some disorder. The invective of Caius Martius against his citizen army raises the mood higher again before they charge. In that battle, Martius, breaking through his own men, follows the fleeing Volscians and goes through the gates into Corioles. They close behind him. Titus Lartius, coming from the other battle, hears what has happened, and speaks an elevated obituary. He (Roy Purcell) knelt downstage in a group of soldiers. One suddenly cries 'Look, sir.' To braying brass in a tremendous tune of victory the big walls parted a little to show, spotlit high up inside the very top of the opening gates, Caius

Martius, blood on his face and arms, smoke about his feet, bowing forward with his bloody sword. His troops below rushed into the city, the walls closing after them.

Scene 5 (Act One, scene five)

The great tune turned to oboe-gentleness as the Roman soldiers came out of the looted city, carrying cushions, plates, spoons, and cloth. Martius, scornful, followed the sheepish looters downstage: he leaves Titus Lartius to make good the city and goes to help Cominius and find Aufidius.

Scene 6 (Act One, scene six)

Quick brass discords and disconnected bursts of sound brought on Cominius with his band of troops, retiring in good order, a light echo lifting his praise of military Rome. A Messenger (Richard Derrington) – who has taken an hour to get there, diverted by 'spies of the Volsces' – reports an earlier stage of the battle. But a bloody figure leaped to the top behind the lower gates, crying 'Come I too late?' – Caius Martius, fearful that he has missed this, other, battle. Alan Howard jumped down from the considerable height to 'clip' Cominius in his arms. Hearing of the battle-positions, and that the Antiates were in the van led by Aufidius himself, he let his excitement rise as he picked the most enthusiastic of the troops who, with shouts alternating with horn-blasts and drums, cried 'Martius! Martius! Martius!' They crowded him and raised him shoulder-high on their spears so that he stood far above them. Howard's rich voice sang over the oboe-tune 'O me alone! Make you a sword of me!' On earth again, he urged his troops away to battle.

Scene 7 (Act One, scene seven)

With the big gates half-closed, the smaller gates open to reveal Titus Lartius, who in echo-effect sent the guard into the captured Corioles. When his Lieutenant was through the big gates, they closed.

Scene 8 (Act One, scene eight)

Immediately, strongly side-lit and in follow-spots, Caius Martius and Aufidius met. Their single combat, each with two heavy steel swords, was noisy, long, fast and very dangerous. The echoing clash of metal and shouts of the two warriors, punctuated by short brass chords, and the rattle of side-drums, was all accompanied by that sweet long oboe version of the tune associated with Martius – his 'love-tune'. Aufidius, eventually just over-matched, lost one sword: Martius, taunting, threw one of his away. They grasped wrists and fought with single swords. Aufidius lost his remaining sword, and stooped for trident and cloak, against Martius with two swords again – both were clearly to be seen as gladiators. Aufidius, worsted again, was suddenly rescued by two Volscian soldiers, to his shame, and to Martius' triumph.

'O me alone! Make you a sword of me!'

Scene 9 (Act One, scene nine)

Martius stood centre-stage, swords crossed over his chest, as Cominius and his
forces entered to praise him. In the battle-scenes, apart from military commentary
and planning, voice had given way to action. Now Cominius reports on his own
reporting, giving a double value to 'voice' in his cameos of the future hearers of
Martius' exploits – senators, patricians, ladies, Tribunes, plebeians all reacting at
one remove. Martius refuses both the extravagance of praise and the offered first
tenth of all the spoil, preferring to take a common share: to which the soldiers
again cried 'Martius, Martius!' interspersed with blasts of horns and drums – to

Aufidius (Charles Dance) and Caius Martius (Alan Howard) in single combat.

the complex revulsion of Caius Martius, who denounces these 'acclamations hyperbolical' from the soldiers. Cominius, however, will not be silenced, and he focuses the experience of the play at this point: he creates the first strong moment of the play's extraordinary interest in names and titles, as part of 'voicing': Caius Martius is acclaimed 'Caius Martius Coriolanus'. Yet the hero's *magnanimitas* almost at once swings to an opposite, for in trying to have freed a poor man of Corioles, he fails to remember that prisoner's name.

Scene 10 (Act One, scene ten)

A bitter Aufidius entered downstage to take position in a close group with four watchful Volscians standing and kneeling, some facing outward, and he, on his own expression of 'emulation', sinking to his knees, his bared head bowed to the floor. Charles Dance rose again among his close soldiers, lifting himself by holding a knee, a shoulder, an arm, an upright spear, his big body against the folds of cloaks and shine of helmets, celebrating his own corruption in his surrender to hyperbolically ignoble means to use his hatred. The near-similarity to Howard's Caius Martius, high on his own soldiers' spears, was striking. This sick and passionate anger, sudden and self-consuming, is the last we see of Aufidius until in scene 21 he welcomes the banished Coriolanus to his own hearth.

FIRST INTERVAL

Scene 11 (Act Two, scene one)

Before the houselights went out, Menenius came on alone and looked and walked slowly about before sitting again centre-stage on his shooting-stick. As the two Tribunes walked past him, in ordinary daylight as it were, the squawk of birds set the subject of augury and therefore of news. This quickly shifts to an analysis of Martius' – and the Tribunes' – pride. The two Tribunes, as the original Stage-Directions indicate, reply precisely in unison occasionally – something that invariably amused audiences. More subtly, the concentration on Martius, on body and speech and exaggeration, is maintained even through the more relaxed prose.

As Menenius is leaving, the Tribunes, Volumnia, Virgilia and Valeria sweep on with news that 'my boy Martius' is coming home. Letters – silent voices – have arrived: he has 'the whole name of the war'; his bodily wounds are particularised, though Menenius makes a little fun over them. As one of the big walls swung forward, trumpets announced Martius' entry at first at the rear and then among his soldiers behind the generals. They call his new name. He greets mother, wife and friends, while the Tribunes in the background greet the soldiers, their citizen friends, before he is swept on formally to the Capitol, the two leaves of the big gates changing position grandly as he does so.

'You are a pair of strange ones'. Menenius (Graham Crowden), Junius Brutus (Oliver Ford-Davies) and Sicinius Velutus (John Burgess).

Brutus and Sicinius are left. Brutus looked after the departing triumph and called in high terms his anger – making his own small cameos of bodies all involved in seeing and welcoming this one man. They are alarmed: 'On the sudden / I warrant him consul.'

Scene 12 (Act Two, scene two)

A Parliamentary division-bell punctuated the scene-change. The seven citizens carried five black-cushioned benches downstage and chattered as they set them three and two for the Senate. (This was the only major re-assignment of lines in the production: Folio gives the lines to two Officers.) The citizens were thus seen struggling with puzzling and conflicting notions about Coriolanus' attitude to themselves and how worthy he might be of their support. As the bell rang again, the citizens left; the robed Senators brought in the bare-armed, scarred and grossly-uncomfortable Coriolanus. Menenius introduces 'the main point of this our after-meeting' which is to reward Coriolanus. The hero rose to leave, and was pushed down by Menenius. As at Westminster, in the debate that followed, as each speaker rose his opponent sat. The triple conflict was between senators, calmly and traditionally applauding by gently slapping their benches – to Coriolanus' alarm: the Tribunes, over-sensitive to his attitude to the people; and Coriolanus himself, made even more touchy and fretful by all this voicing of deeds. Cominius, set to speak formally, admits that he will 'lack voice': Bernard Brown, developing the long account of Coriolanus at Corioles, showed Cominius' agitation in his treatment of the horrors of the warfare he was describing, and was twice checked lest he broke his control completely. Coriolanus had withdrawn, and stood aside facing upstage. As Cominius' heated description grew, three giant shadows of the warrior appeared on the back wall. Coriolanus is called back

The basic set for the Senate scene, scene 12. Only the benches were lit.

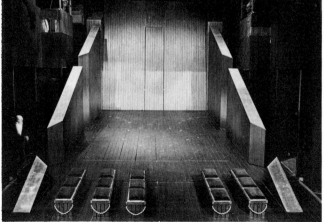

Coriolanus (Alan Howard) in the gown of humility, with Menenius (Graham Crowden).

for confirmation of his consulship. Now he only has to speak to the people. This he instantly asks to be excused, to the sharp disapproval of the Tribunes, whose instant 'Sir, the people / Must have their voices; neither will they bate / One jot of ceremony' stands as one of the keys to this play. Coriolanus' reply, a metaphor of stage-acting, sets going another constellation of meanings in the relation of speech and acting. The senators and Coriolanus leave; the Tribunes, left behind, briefly gather together their understanding of what Coriolanus will do, and follow to the market-place.

Scene 13 (Act Two, scene three)

The two walls on one side came together to make a projecting V-shape. All the cushions and three of the benches were removed, and two put together to make a platform in the market-place. The Citizens stood centre-stage arguing their own rights and Coriolanus' worthiness, with some good-humour, (and some minor re-assignment of speeches). Third Citizen (Arthur Whybrow) was emerging as a comic philosopher, and Sixth (Ron Cook) as the young simpleton. The majority agrees to give Caius Martius the required 'voices', even with some admiration. In

'Lay a fault on us, your tribunes'. Junius Brutus (Oliver Ford-Davies), Sicinius Velutus (John Burgess) with Citizens.

a crude white linen gown, constantly fiddling with a linen belt knotted at the front, pushed on by Menenius from up-stage darkness into light on the platform, came Coriolanus. Howard demonstrated extreme distaste, and some nervous wit, both before and during the engagement with the Citizens. In his honesty of purpose, he made no attempt to win them by dissembling. This cutting truthfulness has already confused the Citizens, and will continue to disturb them here. The orchestration of Alan Howard's voice began to give fuller tones to the word 'voices' itself, so that after his short soliloquy, and its comic-despairing conclusion, 'I am half through; the one part suffered, the other will I do', he began to intone on two notes the two syllables of the world 'voi-ces' in its seven occurrences in as many lines, causing consternation to the citizens, and greater point to Third Citizen's earlier remark 'But this is something odd.' (The Tribunes had stood in the cross-light upstage checking, as each Citizen went forward, who represented each tribe.) On Coriolanus' hasty summons to the Senate House for final confirmation of his consulship, it is not difficult for the Tribunes, while appearing no more than investigative, to suggest that the Citizens had been insulted and manipulated.

They sat in despair at opposite ends of the platform, the Citizens grouping themselves round their white-gowned figures, recognising the enormity of what they had done, their voices reduced now to a silence of impotence. Out of that stillness, Third Citizen's timid voice emerged, 'He's not confirmed; we may deny him yet.' The group rapidly plotted mass retraction in all Rome, guided by the Tribunes in how to make it seem their own idea, even against their own Tribunes' advice. These, left for a moment alone, realise that now they need only wait, for a greater mutiny still.

Scene 14 (Act Three, scene one)

Cornets. Enter CORIOLANUS, MENENIUS, all the Gentry. COMINIUS, TITUS LARTIUS, and other Senators is Folio's Stage-Direction. They stood grandly centre-stage, Caius Martius in his new robes as Consul, with voices strong and stances Olympian as Coriolanus asks for news of Aufidius and what he had said. Strolling downstage, passing by the Tribunes' upraised arms commanding him to stop, at first coolly in control, Howard was quickly angered by the denial of his confirmation by the people. Coriolanus' restless rage comes from his anxiety for the future of Rome from any inch of giving way to the 'mutable, rank-scented meinie'. Sicinius' comment on him,

It is a mind

That shall remain a poison where it is,

Not poison any further,

'Down with that sword'. Left to right: Junius Brutus (Oliver Ford-Davies), Third Roman Citizen (Arthur Whybrow), Second Roman Citizen (Philip Dunbar), Seventh Roman Citizen (Iain Mitchell), Coriolanus (Alan Howard), Menenius (Graham Crowden), First Roman Senator (Paul Imbusch), Sixth Roman Citizen (Ron Cook), Second Roman Senator (Mike Hall), Titus Lartius (Roy Purcell), Cominius (Bernard Brown).

was answered by Howard's tremendous *'Shall? . . . remain?'* and the rolled 'r' on 'Hear you this Triton of the Minnows'.

From this point the scene builds both in the violence of the conflict and the absolute domination of Coriolanus' strong voice, against which the Tribunes, and presently the plebeians too, can only make emotive noises. Howard in full voice gave both high rage and full clarity; the far-sighted passion of a man of an absolute authority amounting to genius who sees the dangers of opposition from fickle, pusillanimous folly, especially when that opposition is worked up by Tribunes. Sicinius was flung to the ground. The people chanted slogans. Howard strode round the stage examining the walls, easily parting the crowd, stopping suddenly front of stage when challenged with arrest, freezing the violent figures into a steely crescent before him with the authority of his warrior-stance. But out of the silent, still moment Menenius, father-figure, found an even higher authority, quietly commanding 'Down with that sword' – and being, a little petulantly, obeyed. Under Brutus' authoritative 'Lay hands upon him', the crowd made another assault. The Aedile (Pat Connell) was pushed forward by the Tribunes. Howard, leaving, struck the Aedile, strode through the crowd and, centre-stage, took another stance. The rabble leave to get weapons. Coriolanus is persuaded to withdraw. Menenius' comment keeps the tension high in its hyperbole,

> He would not flatter Neptune for his trident
> Or Jove for's power to thunder.

The rabble return and are further worked up by the Tribunes. Menenius calms the outrage just sufficiently for acceptance of his promise to bring Coriolanus

> Where he shall answer by a lawful form,
> In peace, to his utmost peril.

Scene 15 (Act Three, scene two)

Out of darkness, a single narrow beam of light from stage-level, far at the front, illuminated the black back wall, through a flap in which strode Coriolanus, his six lines of defiance accompanied by a monstrous, growing shadow of himself as he walked forward, – a moment of Greek tragedy. On 'I muse my mother/Does not approve me further' Howard changed key to domestic irony. His mother entered far upstage by the same door, paused, and in near-darkness approached from behind. Menenius with two senators and Cominius join them, but Volumnia's persuasion dominates the scene. Her son is to dissemble, like an actor: Cominius even adds 'Come, come, we'll prompt you.' Coriolanus visualises, grotesquely, how to act against his nature: Howard became more bizarre, on his knees, head askew, with a rictus of total vacancy, until in a roar of rage he rose on 'I will not do it!' Volumnia's following absolute dismissal of him in his pride led to his mother-caressing submission. Cominius recommends mildness: Coriolanus, unbuckling his sword, accepts. The last word of the scene, his second 'mildly', Howard spat ferociously at the audience before flinging his sword into the wings and striding off.

Scene 16 (Act Three, scene three)

The two Tribunes shuffled on down-stage carrying between them a black trestle table and a bench with papers, Brutus' satchel and, now, Sicinius' briefcase too. They are, in several senses, setting up their office, to 'try' Coriolanus (Hands called this scene the 'kangaroo court'). They plan to 'put him to choler straight', and instruct the Aedile in the cues for the peoples' cry of 'Fine!' or 'Death!'

Coriolanus, entering with the patricians, begins well, Howard with obvious difficulty not exploding at Sicinius' 'shall'. But Sicinius' word 'traitor' does move him, and he is roused to furious verbal attack, rising through hyperbole. The people, on cue, chanted softly 'To th'rock, to th'rock with him'. The Tribunes have the scene excellently in hand. They built him to further rage, carefully sifting their papers for the correct one, formally reading in legal tones 'For that he has / As much as in him lies . . .' their sentence of instant banishment. Cominius' attempts are stonewalled by a *fait accompli.* The people chant repeatedly, 'It shall be so, It shall be so' steadily advancing on Coriolanus until he is forced to do something physical.

Howard in two strides seized the table and raised it above his head on 'You common cry of curs', scattering and freezing everything on stage, and, as punctuation for 'I . . . banish . . . *you*', flinging the table powerfully down, and sending into the shocked silence that the crash caused 'And here remain with your uncertainty'. During Howard's next ten lines he took off his official cloak and flung it down as he backed upstage, his last line mounting with power to the tremendous climax: 'There is . . . a *world* . . . ELSE-WHERE!'

Out of the silence First Citizen moved a step, and in an incredulous small voice said 'The people's enemy is gone!' The stage erupted in a crescendo of action as the shouting and dancing plebeians, hugging each other and their Tribunes, chairing one of them, celebrated their freedom. They left riotously centre-stage.

Scene 17 (Act Four, scene one)

While they were still noisily leaving, one large gate and one smaller gate swung in, and Coriolanus, travel-cloaked, began his farewells to his weeping wife and mother, and Menenius and Cominius. Howard played an easy Stoic acceptance, spurning arrangements for keeping in contact. He made a clean, swift exit through the great gates upstage, leaving his wife, arms high, her body held against the closed doors.

Scene 18 (Act Four, scene two)

Downstage the Tribunes emerged to pick up their scattered papers. Coriolanus' wife, mother and friend came downstage towards them, the smaller gates closing the space behind them, making encounter with the Tribunes unavoidable. Volumnia unburdened at them her grief and despair, now not quite human ('Are you mankind?' the Tribunes ask her). She takes the lamenting Virgilia with her. Menenius, alone on a darkening stage, quietly ended the sequence with his slow and grieving 'Fie, fie, fie'.

SECOND INTERVAL

Scene 19 *(Act Four, scene three)*

A diagonal in strange light made by two walls with a mysterious central gap was a street where two cloaked and hooded figures came across each other in a secret darkness – Volscian territory, we discover, and both men are spies. One is a Roman senator, no less, in Volscian pay, familiar as he removed his hood. Coriolanus' banishment is welcome news in Antium, where an army is already in readiness for an attack on Roman territory.

Scene 20 *(Act Four, scene four)*

From the gap between the walls appeared a barefoot, humble figure with a staff,

Coriolanus (Alan Howard) with Aufidius (Charles Dance).

First and Second Volscian Citizens (David Hobbs and Bille Brown) praise
Coriolanus.

so enwrapped in a black cloak and hood as to seem skinny and insignificant
beneath. '*Enter CORIOLANUS in mean apparel, disguised and muffled*'. In his two
soliloquies, separated by the discovery that he is outside Aufidius' house,
Coriolanus comments on his previous butchery in Antium: 'City / 'Tis I that made
thy widows' and the extremity of reversal of feeling, where love can turn to hate,
and hate to love, in an hour. Coriolanus will try Aufidius: 'If he give me way / I'll
do his country service.'

Scene 21 (Act Four, scene five)

Coriolanus, in light from a follow-spot high above him, is now passed and
re-passed by servants who send for their great master. Their encounter, watched
by motionless, seated attendants, (David Hobbs and Bille Brown) was a restrained
dialogue of love, Aufidius' account of his dreaming of Coriolanus, his 'nightly . . .
encounters' being given silent answering recognition by Howard.

After they have gone in together, the admiring servants rhapsodise over what
they have seen, building Coriolanus to god-like dimensions beyond the power of
words. They hear of Coriolanus' welcome by the Volscian Senators, and that he
will share with Aufidius the lead in an attack on Roman territory immediately.
The servants praise war: sweet music signalled both the end of the feast and the
charms of war, as on 'they are rising, they are rising' the servants rushed jubil-
antly in.

Scene 22 (Act Four, scene six)

The walls opened to a clear stage in full light as Sicinius and Brutus, taking the air,
as it were, on a balmy day, strolled easily downstage. But their talk, even in his

absolute absence, is of Coriolanus. A meeting with Menenius does not disturb them. Contented citizens drifted across the stage, greeting the Tribunes with rather bucolic complacency. Alone with Menenius, the Tribunes reach a still point of perfect rest in self-satisfaction, as all dramatic movement stopped on Oliver Ford-Davies' 'Rome / Sits safe . . . and still . . . without him.'

At once the Aedile enters with the rumour that two Volscian armies have invaded Roman territories, and further entries rapidly build to the certainty that 'a fearful army, led by Caius Martius' is destroying all before them. Cominius recognises the consequences, for 'He is their god'; even Aufidius takes his commands. The citizens spinelessly revolt and turn against the Tribunes: 'though we willingly consented to his banishment, yet it was gainst our will'.

Scene 23 (Act Four, scene seven)

To a clanging of percussion, Aufidius met his Lieutenant in strong follow-spots in the darkness. He appears reluctant, but he is not difficult to persuade that he wishes to destroy Caius Martius, and he obliquely reasserts it in a curious, unexpected soliloquy.

Scene 24 (Act Five, scene one)

Menenius is under persuasion by the Tribunes to visit Coriolanus and plead: he convinces himself that Cominius failed because Coriolanus 'had not dined'. Cominius, when Menenius has left, and now unexpectedly joined with the Tribunes, re-asserts his good reason for knowing that he will fail too.

Scene 25 (Act Five, scene two)

Powerful drum-beats, military-camp search-lights in the darkness, and two confident Volscian sentries hold back Menenius with their spears. His arguments all fail: down the low beam of light from the front strides Caius Martius, accompanied by Aufidius, asking in the words of the first scene, 'What's the *matter?*' Coriolanus, now in blood-red leather and battle-gear, a fully armed Volscian commander, with his word 'Away!' strikes to the heart of Menenius, who has even followed him some way on his knees: Coriolanus' disregard is total, though he has prepared a scroll, which, without looking, he thrust at Menenius. The sentries taunt, but Menenius can summon some dignity for a Roman departure.

Scene 26 (Act Five, scene three)

Through the upstage doors came the two commanders, again with their Lieutenant (Peter Tullo), all moving rapidly forward as Coriolanus plans the attack on Rome for the following day. Aufidius notes his rebuttal of all suits from Rome; Coriolanus even takes some pride in having rejected Menenius. The two Volscian sentries shouted 'Stay!' Howard, looking forward, described the entry of his wife, his mother and his son, with Valeria, far behind him.

Howard's commentary on himself took on a private, low-voiced desperation in hearing his wife speak, as

> Like a dull actor now
> I have forgot my part and I am out,
> Even to a full disgrace.

His kiss of reunion 'Long as my exile, sweet as my revenge' spoke of a full erotic history. He greets his mother, both kneeling, then his neighbour, then his 'poor epitome', his little son. He grants at least a hearing.

The scene is Volumnia's, and the emphasis of light shifted to her, away from the motionless Volscians and the statuesque other Romans. Maxine Audley built it rapidly in emotional range of voice (she is clearly the mother of this Coriolanus). Young Martius (Stephen Humphries, or Paul Basson) stood for his line of defiance down-stage a pace, chin forward in a familiar *moue*: 'one on's father's moods' indeed.

Coriolanus made to go, but Volumnia was not yet in her stride: her main case is honour for either side in showing mercy. As the appeal builds, she calls the deputation to kneel again, and then is silent. Maxine Audley rose and moved forward to face Alan Howard. He, in an instant movement, with a military snap, clasped her hand to his breast and gazed on her. Howard held a long silence,

The Pleading scene. Virgilia (Jill Baker), Coriolanus (Alan Howard), Young Martius (Stephen Humphries), Valeria (Ruth Rosen) and Volumnia (Maxine Audley).

sometimes of forty-four seconds, usually well over thirty, until, tears rolling down his cheeks, he broke. 'O mother, mother, / What have you done?'

It is the hero's moment of tragic recognition. 'Oh / You have won a happy victory to Rome. But for your son . . . most mortal to him. But let it come!' As the Roman group in sculptural closeness moved off stage to slow music of horn and cor anglais, Aufidius expresses triumph.

Scene 27 (*Act Five, scene four*)

In Rome, a sobered Menenius meets a lonely Sicinius. Menenius magnifies Coriolanus, 'He wants nothing of a god but eternity' but sees accurately: Sicinius' 'The gods be good unto us' gets a tart retort, 'No, in such a case the gods will not be good unto us . . .'. Second and Third Citizens warn Sicinius to flee, as his fellow Tribune has just been attacked; worse is to follow if the ladies do not succeed. First Citizen's tremendous shout of 'Good news, good news! The ladies have prevailed' is soon pointed by a dancing, braying tune of joy. Sicinius is snubbed by First Citizen.

Scene 28 (*Act Five, scene five*)

Large processional music brought on Cominius and Senators, Virgilia and Valeria, and then Volumnia with Young Martius, a cloak around him. Cominius' appeal for shouts of welcome received muted words only as the citizens saw what Volumnia was doing, for at the climax of the music she flung off Young Martius' cloak to show him, hands crossed over a sword, black leather armour and defiant chin, the young image of his father. Clearly she is going to repeat the process of a special fanatical upbringing all over again.

Scene 29 (*Act Five, scene six*)

Aufidius, returning to his own city, had no such triumph; he simply slipped on stage, gave an account of recent events for the lords, and greeted his own soldier-conspirators. Aufidius easily convinces himself he is wronged. A sudden burst of triumphant music underlines the difference between the commanders.

Howard's entry from the far back wall, to tremendous martial music from the whole brass and full light, follow-spots tracking him step by step downstage, was given high power by the moving of the greater and the lesser walls each side, together, to make a new, and extraordinarily powerful, stage-shape, so that Howard seemed to enter between two black cliffs. Precisely at the climax of the music he placed his sword before his feet on the ground, centre-stage. His account of his action is interrupted by the words of Aufidius, 'traitor', 'Martius', 'boy of tears': Howard, at that, gave a voiced, strong inward-breathing gasp, while the soldiers took sudden defensive stance. Howard's next two words at great volume unleashed great action – '*Mea* . . . *sure* . . . *less LIAR!*' His passion rose as he repeated 'Boy!' and he taunted the surrounding soldiers:

The killing.

> Cut me to pieces, Volsces; men and lads,
> Stain all your edges on me. 'Boy'! False hound!
> If you have writ your annals true, 'tis there
> That, like an eagle in a dove-cot, I
> Fluttered your Volscians in Corioles.
> Alone I did it. 'Boy!'

Aufidius' cry 'Let him die for it' was answered by Volscian shouts. Aufidius picked up Coriolanus' sword. Howard turned downstage in the ring of spears and cried in a great voice

> O that I had him
> With six Aufidiuses or more – his tribe,
> To use my lawful sword

and flung himself on his own sword in Aufidius' hands. Mortally wounded, he cried 'Kill, kill', fists clenched, staggering up-stage a pace or two, falling face down amid the sudden rush of jabbing spears and trampling feet. The shocked lords with great shouts protested; Aufidius' excuse sounds lame, and 'My rage is gone, / And I am struck with sorrow . . .'

> Though in this city he
> Hath widowed and unchilded many a one
> Which to this hour bewail the injury
> Yet he shall have a noble memory.
> Assist.

The body of Coriolanus is borne off.

Volscian soldiers shouldered the body and to a funeral march carried it up-stage while to that sad music a slow procession of all the Romans, led by the Tribunes, filed round the darkening stage and lined the ceremonial farewell in decreasing brightness round the body of Coriolanus.

Three

Paris II

The second performance in Paris became part of the active mythology of the tour. With one sharp exception, everything went wonderfully well, and the packed house responded with warmth and delight. The actors were relaxed and happy, all the nervousness of the previous night having gone. Alan, however found follow-spots in his eyes in the duel (the angle was slightly lower than it had been in the Aldwych), and he incorporated shouted protests into his fight-noises. There was some feeling back-stage that though the fight should not have been made more dangerous than it actually was, protest also should not have been made in front of the audience. The matter was debated by the company with academic thoroughness for some days.

I asked Alan about his first entry, where I had seen him as a gladiator. 'Terry and I worried at that. Caius Martius has the feeling of being a bullfighter, certainly a gladiator. Things are going wrong because nothing is happening. These are the opening moments of a person caught by inactivity, looking for trouble, wanting to challenge and have a bash, wanting a wall to hit the ball against, wanting to keep

Scene 1. Caius Martius (Alan Howard) in scorn of the Citizens with Menenius (Graham Crowden).

fresh and alive and vital his hatred for Aufidius, to keep it sharp. So he tries to get the Citizens to fulfil that sort of rôle, making purity of hate, something non-compromising. If they hate him as he hates them, then . . .'

Later, of the election of the Tribunes, Alan noted that Coriolanus can't get on with them, can't stand compromise, so his ferocity against the Citizens is hugely tempered by the news. He feels that everything will now start to be compromise, to be wheeling and dealing; nothing will be straight. The Citizens, who are the soldiers, are, though out of his class, valiant, and they can be together when fighting, when it is not black market or usury. 'But with the Tribunes, there will be dealing in terms of people's inadequacy: he and they are on a collision course, and they have an equally bad effect on each other – Brutus refers to their physical revulsion; Shakespeare goes into smells, and so on . . .'

Of Volumnia, Alan said that she was always trying to get him to capitulate, to use his filial affection to make him subservient. Though manipulative, she was also obtuse, he felt. 'The first thing she says to him after his return is "Nay, *my* good soldier, up". She doesn't seem to have any awareness of his not wanting that, not always wanting to be her creation, so he breaks that first meeting off. I don't think he wants things to be said. The growing problem in terms of his marriage is how to keep some normal relationship with his mother. From the beginning of the play she has not done anything to help. Later, he seems to have to be twelve sons, all rolled into one. He is not completely unaware of what he is lacking from his mother. No father is ever mentioned. He is living with three women – I kept that at the back of my mind. He values silence, he wants to be alone. So his relationship with his wife, Virgilia, is very powerful and extraordinary. Jill got an awful lot out of the part.'

Terry spoke warmly to the cast on stage after the show and then met all the technical staff for a conference in the Green Room. To an outsider, again, it seemed a remarkable way of life that not only involved sitting and working together at one in the morning, but that also everyone present could refer to and agree to alter, from memory, details expressed largely in numbers through three and a half hours of recollected performance.

Terry was more than welcome: his presence the first day, most of the company felt very strongly, would have prevented some of the trouble, reduced the anxieties, and removed the strain. He had set out from London, but a fire on the motorway had severely delayed his taxi and he had missed his plane, and gave up the idea of ever getting to Paris that first night.

Directing this *Coriolanus* he was at that pont in his career where international success had opened many possibilities to someone still young (thirty-eight) and able to take them all. A dozen years with the RSC had included five major Shakespearean productions up to 1974 at Stratford and the Aldwych, one of his first, the triumphant *Merry Wives* of 1968, being brought back seven years later –

this sort of extremely rare revival tending to happen to a Hands production. His scope outside Shakespeare in that time showed his own range, and that of the Company: the Cuban play *The Criminals; Women Beware Women; The Balcony; The Man of Mode; Murder in the Cathedral; The Bewitched* – all main-house RSC productions. In the centenary 1975 season at Stratford he directed all four productions – the revived *Merry Wives,* the two *Henry 4* plays and *Henry 5*: his Hal was Alan Howard. That *Henry 5* toured Britain and Europe, in 1976 went to New York as the official British Theatre offering for the American bi-centennial celebrations, and was revived in 1977 and 1978 in Stratford and at the Aldwych.

His production of all three *Henry 6* plays at Stratford in 1977 was a significant event in theatrical history: according to all available records, these three plays had never been seen in their entirety since Shakespeare's day, though all Europe, and the USA, had known them in strange re-writings, curiosities which maintained the universal prejudice that such 'early' plays of Shakespeare could not possibly be good. Hands and his team showed that, with a full text and a fully-professional cast, they were stunningly successful. The plays transferred to the Aldwych, and Hands won two awards. Awards also followed two of his French-language productions of Shakespeare, and of Corneille and T. S. Eliot at the Comédie Française where he was Consultant Director from 1975 to 1978. His *Richard 3* and *Twelfth Night* at the Comédie were two of his greatest successes. His two recent German-language Shakespeare productions at the Burgtheater in Vienna were the sell-outs of the season. His present Covent Garden *Parsifal*, with Solti, is only one of several opera invitations, and the official French Opera offering to the USA for the American bi-centennial celebrations was his *Otello* with the Paris Opera.

His very successes, however, have made him enemies, and his present popularity in most of Paris is countered by dislike in certain places there which does not distress him at all. The Paris press polarises politically. Terry is a Comédie Française man, and therefore attracts the same labels as its Director, Pierre Dux. The Comédie, because it is a large organisation with a vast budget, is said by the Left to be a Right-Wing organisation. So the Left in Paris do not like the Comédie; so they are suspicious of Terry Hands. Theatre-politics, which partly cuts across national politics, each complicating the other, causes further strong reactions. The acclaim in Paris for the foreigner in his first work can quickly turn sour. The enormous success of Hands' *Murder in the Cathedral* for the Comédie in 1978 created a cabal of critics against him, though there were those in Paris who put it that the best work Pierre Dux ever did was to invite Terry Hands. So the critics of several papers, I was told, including *Le Monde*, a Marxist paper, of course, would decide to hate Terry Hands' *Coriolanus* before they arrived to see it. Terry said to me somewhat ruefully that though he himself was a little more Left than Right, he had to admit that throughout Europe the Conservative press tended to be more generous in its praise. The reaction of the public, in fact, largely independent of the press, has been most generous of all. The audiences for *Murder in the Cathedral*,

Graham Crowden and Bernard Brown.

during the worst winter Paris had known for many decades, in a theatre that rarely achieved more than 45 per cent attendance, had kept a steady 95 per cent: such audiences knew that they would be sure of a rich theatrical experience.

From Graham Crowden's Journal. Thursday. Walked over to the Opera House to find out about tickets for *Cosi Fan Tutti.* Met an actor/designer – very French – charming – he'd seen the play – You play Menenius, *non*? – Yes, I do – Good, very nice, I like it – Thankyou – Very nice. We walked over Pont Neuf together. He's going to design the sets for *King Lear* with Jean Marais. He said – Shakespeare marvellous playwright – very nice – *King Lear* good play. I concurred. My French he managed to follow – but I did start to project at him, to which he said 'I understand English better than she is when I speak it'. Very charming. Must not shout at foreigners. After all it's their city and language.

During the run of our performances in Paris, the press, with one exception, remained enthusiastic. *L'Aurore* on the Thursday, with a neat and witty little cartoon of Alan, Maxine and Graham, said how necessary it was to have two intervals, less for the actors, whose rhythms of breathing seemed unaffected by '*les plus violents orages tragiques*', than for the audience, constrained, for four hours by the clock, to confront their English with that of Shakespeare.

'Happily the presentation by Terry Hands is free of the political accretions which the continental producers following Brecht have thought fit to encumber it with . . . The hero is not fascist because he despises the people; he also despises the patricians and the senators . . . 'The enemy changes, and the General is susceptible to the pleas of his wife and mother. Unlike the notices in other cities – particularly in Germany – the Paris press was appreciative of the play as a whole. Thus the heart of the review in *L'Aurore* is an appreciation of the great talent in the '*rôles secondaires*' played by actors '*à l'aise dans leur texte*'. In particular, John Burgess and Oliver Ford-Davies are noted with appreciation. 'All their feelings can be read in their faces, which are so much lived-in that one has the illusion of being able to understand even if one cannot receive the English.' Maxine Audley, remembered as a young leading lady at the *Théâtre des Nations* in the fifties, has since taken on the true mask of the *'tragédienne'*. Alan Howard is less vocally extreme than in *Henry 5*: '*Instrument et instrumentiste, il rend à miracle la musique de l'orchestre Shakespearien.*' He has become a true rival for Olivier.

As expected, the Marxist *Le Monde* quibbled. Terry Hands, said Michel Cournot, has made a place for himself at the Comédie Française where a faithful audience applauds him. He has now put his *Coriolanus* in the inside of a giant box made of planks of pine painted black . . . everything is black, even the lighting, which uses spots like a music-hall, and everything moves towards fixed groups like funerary statuary, making touching tableaux. The old-fashioned recitation of Shakespeare with 'tonalities bronzed like an old portable harmonium' is, between friends, he says, almost a national sport. Is Coriolanus *'un fifils à sa maman'* or a Colonel wanting blood, or what? We shall never know, as the interpretation remains wide open. The trouble is, concludes Cournot, that Alan Howard, though he has many tricks up his sleeve and plays games with his arms like a featherweight boxer, simply hasn't got what it takes: he lacks 'that mysterious flame which elevates a rare phenomenon, equal to the genius of Shakespeare'.

France Soir, without such an obviously personal axe to grind as Cournot, went instead for literary whimsy about the Bard of the Odéon, including a rather mysterious reference to a jolly play about 'the future Henry 4', but it was lavish in its all-round praise: the RSC has carried off a triumph. *Le Matin* made a double feature: the first part, a review under the heading 'The tragedy of a hero trapped by a new form of fatality – the class-struggle', gave particular appreciation of the speaking. The second part was an interview with Alan Howard, summarised in Howard's words 'Neither in life nor in Shakespeare should one look for direction from above.' The actor's role is a whole way of life: Howard made a strong plea for not making rigid concepts about Shakespeare, echoing Terry Hands' directive to every member of the company, actors and technicians alike, 'make it yours'.

As Jean-Jacques Courtier had splendidly affirmed, Hands and Howard clearly have a big following in Paris. What struck me was the vigour, the intelligence and the acuteness of interest of the audience that the RSC attracted. They were there to see outstanding theatre, a profound play profoundly performed. Their final applause included many 'Bravos': Balbine Huet of the Odéon told me that they were not at all common at the theatre. Early on those chill over-cast April evenings, a queue of young people under the arches along one side of the Odéon looked like the familiar London crowd outside the Albert Hall in summer for the Proms: predominantly young, knowing, enthusiastic. They were waiting for access to the upper levels of the theatre. Balbine took me to see where they would be sitting. The Odéon is very comfortable, at the lower levels, in the equivalent to the stalls, circle and gallery; the next two levels are a little less pleasant. The

Queuing at the Odéon for the Amphitheatre.

deuxième balcon, the third level above the ground, suffers from having in it three follow-spot operators who cannot help making a little noise, and it is not terribly comfortable. It is normally rejected by people at the ticket-office. There is, however, an even higher fourth level, the *Amphithéâtre*. From the stage, one sees only dark shallow arches under the ceiling, apparently for decoration: but behind them there are hard wooden benches. The view is very limited: even if you see through an arch, rather than simply listen from behind a four-foot wide pillar, you look down almost vertically on to the stage: and it is very hot. The Odéon, naturally, does not try to press those fifty or so places on to the public, and reckons a capacity of nine hundred and fifteen without them; on the second night of *Coriolanus*, the audience was nine hundred and forty-five – the *Amphithéâtre* was well filled. On Friday and Saturday there were nine hundred and thirty-seven and nine hundred and thirty-four. One night I sat for a while among those devotees, on a second-row bench. The acoustics were startling: I stood and craned and stretched, and for a moment got an Olympian view of the tops of some heads on about half the stage. For seats like these was that queue forming, for *Coriolanus*.

Terry left early on Thursday morning. On the technical side, Thursday evening's performance again represented a triumph over unexpected difficulties. In the afternoon, in the middle of a lighting session, the Chief Electrician at the Odéon got word that one of his follow-spot operators had been mugged in the Métro and was in hospital with head injuries. This was sad, and serious. Practically, it meant calamity for the evening performance. It happened that Mike Taylor, who was to replace Basher in Vienna when he went off to light *Cymbeline* in Stratford, had come to Paris to talk to Basher and to re-learn the show which he hadn't been on since a year before in Newcastle. So Mike could do the follow-spot; except that as he didn't speak French, he would also have to have cues in English. The other regular English follow-spot operator, Garry, now knew the show so well that he hadn't needed cues after the first night, so Di had been able to relax and give follow-spot cues only in French. But that night she had, in addition to everything else, to cue a new follow-spot operator in English. 'Which' she said cheerfully afterwards, 'was difficult.'

As I came through the back-stage corridors soon after the start, I was struck again by the stately, careful tread of actors going on and off stage, thinking, calm. Philips's voice over the tannoy I found reassuringly normal – I, now a back-stage veteran of two whole performances. 'Stand by please for scene three. Scene three stand by. Your calls Miss Audley, Miss Baker, Miss Morris and Miss Rosen. Miss Audley, Miss Baker, Miss Morris, Miss Rosen, your calls. Props stand by cue one. Musicians stand by cues three to six. Props staff stand by please for cue one. Musicians stand by cues three to six . . .' I crept down behind the stage and along towards the front. Behind a curtain, further forward, Di's voice was just audible, cueing the lights in a technical French meaning little to an outsider:

'*Attention poursuite effet deux . . . Attention la console effet seize à vingt-six . . . la console effet seize – go! . . . La console effet dix-sept et poursuites – go! Attention poursuite effet trois . . . La console effet dix-huit, et les poursuites effet trois toute ensemble – go! Attention Christophe pour couper, attention effet quatre. . . .*'

During the main interval of that performance I talked to some of the audience. They were excited and fairly stunned by the clarity of the experience, even those with little English having grasped the heart of what was happening. Alan's power, and the fulness of the rôles round him, were always commented on with energy, and indeed passion. I found myself in the presence of an audience of unusual character, highly intelligent, casually well-dressed, volubly enjoying themselves, and a-buzz about the play. For such an audience was *Hamlet* written, I felt.

Author's journal. Friday. This morning I woke so knotted with exhaustion and nervous tension that I couldn't take a deep breath. Four nights with only a few hours' sleep, and the corporate crises and tensions of four long days, from airport delays to muggings, from bad-tempers to bad colds, from missed meals to steaks at 2 am., had screwed my solar plexus into a tight tangle. Unlike every single other person in this enterprise, I don't share the experience of emotional discharge in the performance. My writer's rhythm is infinitely slower, charging up to a release in months not hours.

At breakfast, Pat Connell said that he and Barrie Rutter were going to a Turkish Bath, and I was welcome. It was a very Turkish bath indeed, in the Mosque at the Jardin des Plantes: we had to be careful not to strip right off, which was not permitted. Barrie, an old hand, left drinks to cool in the fountain as we undressed by the raised tesselated platform; going through into the heat was for a moment unbearable: but sitting swooning on the ledge in the nearest I can get to the Lotus position, I felt the tension melting. An hour of Yoga in the heat, of washing, of cold shower, of rubbing dry and I was as supple as a young cat asleep in the sun. Dressed, and stretched out, we drank mint tea, ate oranges, and chattered, while twenty silent Turks lay close on their beds alongside us and listened.

That afternoon there was a conference of the English technical staff in the Green

John Moore at his sound-board.

Room to plan the get-in to Vienna, starting with the problem of the first get-out in Paris on Sunday night to get the lorries on the road by four a.m. That first get-out – and no-one had taken down just this set before – was going to have to be one of the fastest. The back wall and the back two layers of the rostrum were going to have to be dismantled and packed before the ramp could be let down to allow the big doors to open to get anything out of the theatre at all. Hal explained that Terry would land in Vienna at twelve on Tuesday, and be at the theatre by one, and by that time much of the basic lighting work would have had to be finished, because Terry's lighting work would have to stop at four. Uniquely, he reminded everyone, there was in Vienna another show performing the night we arrived. It had been unavoidable, had been carefully planned for, and would not happen again on the tour. The careful planning included the fact that, as the Burgtheater stage is so large, most of the set could be built in the wings.

That meeting was relaxed. English and French crews were working so well together that technically, all agreed, the show was amazing. The actors were tired, and Alan in particular seemed very tired: but the performance was still outstanding, and miracles had been worked. Back-stage understanding was so good that one of the two interpreters had been cancelled. There seemed to be only two slight matters for any correction: the battle was temporarily without its smoke, because the smoke-gun was broken – but one was being borrowed from the Opera; and the matter of getting the carnets stamped for customs clearance from Paris was being attended to, and should soon be settled. There was general

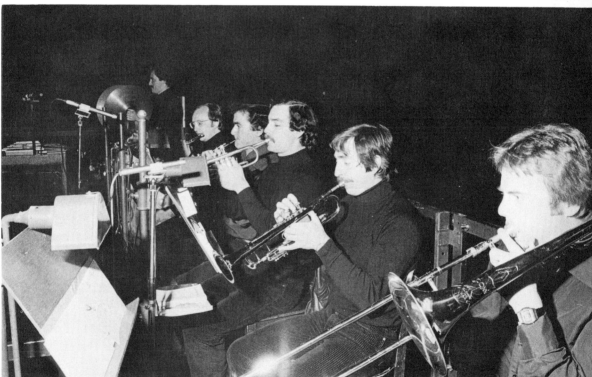

The Musicians on their gantries. Top left to right: Duncan Hollowood, Brian Newman, Peter Whittaker, Nigel Garvey. Bottom left to right: Tony McVey, Christopher Lacey, Nigel Roberts, Roderick Tearle, Peter Cameron, David Hissey.

The ASM (Caroline Howard) at the props table in the wings.

praise for all the French crews and their enthusiasm: the Odéon crew working the big trucks (walls) had got the movements right, twice, precisely, which had never been expected. All was set for a clear run now, to get a good breath for the complexities of Vienna.

Friday 8.15. To collect together my understanding, I made quick notes on what every member of the company was doing, at one time.

In imagination I freeze the action at the moment when, in scene 4, the Roman soldiers have been beaten back by the Volscians, and have been berated by Caius Martius. Visible to the audience are twelve actors, on stage. High in the auditorium, in the *deuxième balcon* are at this point two follow-spot operators, one English (Garry) and one French (joined by a third for the last act). They take their cues from Di over headsets and they are in touch with her through their own mikes. Around the stage, in near-darkness, are many people. Di sits at her desk in a converted lower box, her eyes just above the front of the stage, her fingers at this moment poised over several cue-light switches, including two master-switches – seven red lights are up on her board. She gives over the two mikes follow-spot and 'LX' ('electrics') cues. Philip and his young French equivalent have moved silently into the box for a moment or two to check. (At the start of the performance, Philip, having received front-of-house clearance, had briefly come in to give Di the signal to go.)

Back to back, in fact, with Di's cue-board, but further up-stage, in the wings, is a complicated sound-board, at which sits John Moore, with headphones, a full script, a big Revox tape-deck for echo effects, and red and green cue-lights from Di. His four giant speaker-boxes are hidden inside the black walls of the gantries on either side of the stage. John is at this moment controlling the sound from the mikes used to amplify the instruments in the band above. The long, high gantries, which form the sides of the set, hold each an upper platform on which are the ten musicians, five each side. On one side stands Gordon Kember, Music Director, at a music-stand with red-and-green cue-lights. His white gloves, for conducting, are visible across in the other gantry as well. On each side, at the front of a gantry, stands a French follow-spot operator, each with a head-set, with Jake alongside one of them supervising, and signalling across the gap to the other one.

Below, the Property Master, John O'Mahoney, and the ASM (Assistant Stage Manager) Caroline Howard, have collected cushions, spoons, plates and gold cloth from the props table in the wings and wait by the upstage entrances to give them to the Roman soldiers when they come off, before their next almost immediate entry from 'Corioles'. Behind the back wall stands Lucy, ready for Alan, with a blood-bottle and mirror taken from the quick-change table. Behind the great moving walls, on either side, stand Alistair and Neil and six French stage-hands, ready to move the 'trucks'. Their cue-light is already on red for stand-by. On one side in the wings sits a Fire Officer, (a member of the local fire department), and three or four French stage-hands, quietly and good-humouredly chatting.

Up a vertical steel ladder above the stage-hands is a small cramped room like something out of an older battleship, one wall of which is entirely lighting controls. A TV monitor on an upper corner shows the stage. A small speaker gives Di's voice (there are also two red and green cue-lights, at this moment on red) and she is saying *'Attention la console effet vingt-et-un A.'* Two men stand to work the individual circuit levers and the big master wheels; an older man sits alongside. They follow a written plot in front of them.

Backstage, the tannoy in each corridor, and each room, plays the loud sounds from the stage. In dressing-rooms, actors rest, and adjust costumes, helped if necessary by local dressers. Cynthia Gilman, Wardrobe Assistant and Alan's personal dresser, is in his dressing-room, setting-up for his return, for cleaning and adjustment. Sue Honey, Wardrobe Mistress, is in Maxine's dressing-room, helping her change costume.

In the RSC office, Hal Rogers sits at a desk with Maureen Proud checking accounts. Sue Whitmarsh, the Tutor and chaperone, has just brought in Paul Basson and Stephen Humphries, the Young Martiuses. She will leave one to perform, looked after by Hal, and take the other home to the hotel.

Friday's performance was better than ever. I was very taken by the variety of Alan's methods with a single speech, which I had now seen four times in Paris and four times before. Towards the end of scene 15 Coriolanus' means of inducing himself to act before the plebeians is to take on 'some harlot's spirit'. Howard put on a foolish, mindless bizarreness of appeal to match the grotesque distortions of body in the text, through piping voice, smiles, tears, and tongue, sinking slowly to his knees to combine begging with a harlot's soliciting and both with a parody

The Tutor and Chaperone (Sue Whitmarsh) with the two Young Martiuses (Stephen Humphries and Paul Basson).

of acting, (arms, face, voice, and body all just wrong). Yet he kept a vocal pattern of intense interest, different every night, so that one began to see, lightly touched, each time a completely new range of colours in the palette, as it were. At the same time such folly was in its own way harlot-like, and seductive, and the following tremendous upright 'I will not do't' was a genuine revulsion from something possible. Again I marvelled that though much else was happening, every syllable came across.

Journal: Friday night. Saturday morning. Invited by Paris friends to dinner after the show, and at their pressing invitation took Jill and Graham. We left more or less with the dawn, exhaustions and crises by then belonging somewhere else. Paris cool and clean and stately as we crossed the bridges; I felt Wordsworthian and Westminster Bridge-ish; he had been on his way to France, of course.

On Saturday morning, it was clear to Alan that his cold was very much worse, and that his voice was going. A senior throat-specialist said he had severe infection and laryngitis, that he needed forty-eight hours rest to clear it, gave him a jab of penicillin and left the big decision up to him. That must have been a very hard thing, for Alan works, as everyone knows, phenomenally, and *not* to work is not to be Alan. One hears legends about the few days he has had off the stage for sickness in the past ten years. But the decision was made, not to do the performances Saturday night and Sunday afternoon.

The specialist's appointment had been at the end of Saturday afternoon: it was half past five before work could begin on re-arranging the show, and most of the actors were out in Paris. But there was no alarm: arrangements were routine.

Two notices went up in the Foyer of the Odéon:

> *Par suite d'une indisposition*
> *Alan Howard ne pourra jouer ce soir.*
> *Le rôle de Coriolan sera tenu par*
> *Charles Dance, celui de Aufidius*
> *par Iain Mitchell.*

Charlie, a head taller, kept most of his own costume. Iain wore some of Alan's. The colours weren't always right, but the effect was more than adequate. They managed a fight-rehearsal. The Citizens, as they were found, came in, and they simply readjusted Iain's Seventh Citizen's lines among themselves. Di went to Charlie's and Iain's dressing-rooms for a lines run-through.

The only confusion was with the Odéon stage-management, a misunderstanding which became comic on both sides. Philip asked for the announcement to be given to the audience over the tannoy just before curtain-up, by their stage-manager: the French official, having just arrived and heard only that Alan was ill, could not understand why the British were letting the audience assemble and settle in before telling them the performance was cancelled. It took a while for him to register that the loss of a principal did not mean the loss of the show.

There were limits to what Charles and Iain could do that was original, but they gave fresh readings of great interest. Iain's Aufidius was sinister, devious, reptilian almost – ahead of his own conspirators in Machiavellianism with an evil smile, and a bonny fighter. Charles' Coriolanus was a much less complicated man, with an honest lucidity which added to his tragic stature – a Roman English gentleman caught in an appalling dilemma through his very truth. His 'friends of noble touch' were closer to him than one had seen: Graham reported that whereas Alan, in his haste to get away cleanly at the end of scene 17, would merely brush Menenius' hand with his own on 'Give me thy hand', Charlie took Graham's and held it, a brief moment of force. This performance was clear and compelling: he rightly got tremendous applause, and great cheers. As he came finally off, back-stage the French stage-crew stood and warmly applauded him.

In the café afterwards, I found myself sitting, in the RSC party, next to a young French actress, who told me that she had been moved to tears by Charles' performance, not least by his *'servitude du texte'* when he could have made a personal dash for individualism. Michel Grey in a second notice in *L'Aurore* about

Sunday's performances, with Charles in the afternoon and Alan at night, under the heading *'Deux Coriolan le même jour'*, wrote with exceptional admiration for Charles, taking so readily a crushing rôle, so that one felt *'une émouvante solidarité regnait sur le plateau'*. Grey noted that the RSC was unique in this organisation and skill with understudies – no wonder they have broken box-office records at the Odéon.

I asked Charlie about his reactions. He said that *lucidité* is something he goes for every time: *Coriolanus* is a difficult play, demanding concentration even from English-speakers: for the non-English it needs to be clearer still. Yet he felt that at one level it was a very precise play, and hard to make unclear. In the 'corn-debate' in the middle of scene 14, 'for some-one who professes not to be a good speaker, he makes a very logical coherent argument.' Charlie said that he himself went, for the most part, for the simplest interpretation, though as everyone agreed, at any point Elizabethan language is very full; 'if you bump your head you probably say "damn"; an Elizabethan would curse the door, curse the wood, curse the tree the wood came from, curse the acorn . . .'

Charlie also felt that in Caius Martius there was a warmth which he wanted to bring out – for example, in his great love for Menenius, who calls him 'my son, my son': Charlie felt that they had shared many an embrace, that Caius as a child had many times sat on his knee, been hugged, been loved without demands made in return. 'The greatest love is between those two: "Thy General is my lover," "Yet for I lov'd thee".' Charlie as Coriolanus did make his final handshake with Menenius in scene 17 something strong and direct, because he felt it was signifi-cant as the last time he was ever going to know that hand. He understood Caius Martius' warmth not only to Virgilia, but also in his own private kind of honesty. He tries to do the best he can, and wants no reward, but when he is not fighting there is little else he can do. 'Like Churchill, having got power and the freedom to use it is reward enough: yet secretly he wants to be liked but doesn't know how to get affection. He desperately wants to be understood, and he himself cannot understand how it has happened for example in scene 16 that he has been passed for consul with full voice, and then been dishonoured and taken off again. He genuinely wants to know, and asks "What's the matter?" out of real desperation, for his understanding is stretched to the limit. This gives him some measure of tragic humanity.'

Journal. Sunday morning. My tiny attic room has a table in a dormer window. As I write I look out over the roofs of Paris, Notre Dame on my right, Sacré Coeur gleaming on its hill ahead of me, in – at last – bright sunshine. The big bell of Notre Dame is making the moment romantic: I can't starve in an attic, scribble away among the roof-tops, without Paris making a drama out of it.

The RSC Brass Quintet had been unable to serenade each assembling audience at the Odéon, as planned, because another play was running in the smaller house,

The RSC Brass Quintet blow a fanfare on the roof of the Odéon

starting earlier. But they could blow their hearts out for the Sunday matinée, and they did, and in style too, standing behind a narrow balustrade high up by the tops of the pillars in the gold Foyer, the sound smiting the mirrored walls mightily. They began and ended by ringing their fanfare out over Paris from the leaded roof-top of the theatre, causing cars to halt and cafés to empty with surprise, faces gazing up at the gleaming instruments. The final chord cracked round the Place de l'Odéon like a shot from the artillery of archangels.

Balbine Huet had been concerned to get English-speaking audiences, particularly for the Sunday afternoon – an audience, she explained, normally sluggish and soporific after lunch. Unfortunately a long strike by the Paris Post Offices disrupted her announcements. Yet I was struck by the liveliness of that particular audience. In talking to them in the interval I found, it is true, a larger number than usual of native English, or excellent English-speakers, yet there was still a majority, it seemed, for whom Shakespeare in English was being heard for the first time, and the forcefulness of their expression of admiration came at me in almost vehement French. Alan was back for the evening performance, in rich voice again, and he and the whole cast received long and rapturous curtain-calls.

Journal. Sunday evening. Stood amid helmeted black-caped Roman soldiers, jammed into the room of the Chief Electrician at the Odéon, to watch on French television the first instalment of Lew Grade's *Life of Shakespeare*, rather horribly dubbed into French. The script was made of every cliché in American TV's idea of a Classic Costume Drama Especially The Bard, and one could hear the rustle of dollars every time the sequence changed. The Globe Theatre was insanely small, holding barely three and a half people, rather than the three and a half thousand it actually did. But we all stood there and cheerfully loved it because our own Ron Cook, Sixth Citizen, and Soldier, there with us, was in it, in drag, as Viola in a rehearsal scene from *Twelfth Night*. Everyone in the tiny room busily identified actor friends, and when Ron/Viola got up and walked across a carpet on the 'Globe' stage over the open trap, and so fell through, there was huge happy laughter.

The first minutes of a get-out. Nigel Garvey and Peter Whittaker are lowering valuable timpani while things are being removed all round them. Brian Newman below is reading the insurance policy.

One of the things I had to learn was the usefulness of the 'iron'. Sitting comfortably in the audience when that Safety Curtain comes down for an interval one does not think of what might be going on behind such insulation. When it was down in the main interval of Charlie's first performance on Saturday, there was a cheerful, fairly noisy, rehearsal of the funeral procession, with Philip Dunbar, (Second Citizen) coming in to take Charlie's own place as a bearer so that the sizes remained constant. There were a lot of people on stage, and many movements to co-ordinate quickly, all this happening quite unknown to the audience a few feet away.

Now on Sunday evening, at about ten to midnight, the iron came down as the last applause finished: and the stage was suddenly not a holy place of tragic consummation, but a workshop, as the rapid get-out began. Neil put two plastic buckets on the stage for screws, nuts and bolts. Busy himself, he moved quietly about directing the whole operation. After ten minutes, all the musical instruments were down and packed, with music-stands, mikes and lamps from the gantries. After twenty minutes, the back of the set was hollow, suffering major surgery as I watched. After half an hour, the great walls were down and being folded in on themselves, their ribs removed. I then went to bed. Early next morning I looked in at the stage, and wished I hadn't. The big space had reverted to bare, drab normality.

The lorries were on their way to Vienna, but only after three days of The Great Carnet Saga, which had occupied much of Hal's time. There had been misunderstandings, urgent searches for vanished lorry drivers, dramatic dashes to the Odéon, even more dramatic swoops by taxi to a lorry-park at Versailles by what Maureen called The Heavy Brigade – Alistair, Neil and Jake with a big hammer – and the sensational breaking of the windows of the cabs to get in to find the carnets, which weren't there, while several hundred French workmen building an exhibition on the site took not the slightest notice whatsoever, though the taxi-driver did disappear at the sound of the first blow. Then a frantic dash by all three, still with the hammer, to get to the Champs Elysées by five, in a taxi whose driver refused either to understand or to hurry, and, at five past five, the discovery of the carnets all stamped and ready on an official's desk.

Journal. Monday morning. Going out to buy oranges I meet Graham on the Boulevard St. Michel opposite the Sorbonne. He is not well, but stands in the bitter wind to tell me glorious stories of opera performances. I am conscious, though he isn't, of a small admiring circle forming round us, and cameras come out. There is much clicking and smiling as this tall dramatic presence in Cossack hat and rich grey beard opens his eyes very wide to make a tremendous point at the climax of a tale. He tells me too how he paced the week for the last heavy two-performance day, and was not defeated by his present chill. He has two tricks when very tired or his voice is uncertain. One is to cut very quickly into the cue, which gives time to rest at the beginning of the lines. The other – 'Larry Olivier told me this one – sing it: it makes it different but nobody minds – sing it down the breath.' He felt that Charlie got the *story* across very well.

On the last night in Paris, the RSC Brass Quintet gave a well-advertised concert in the L'Église Saint Merri, a lofty, very ancient church in the older part, across the Seine from the Odéon. Many of the company attended, and so did over three hundred others. The brass sounds, and indeed the announcements of each piece, got gloriously lost in the high mediaeval stone vaulting. I have rarely heard such live acoustics; but the occasion was a good one, and the audience was unusual, being strangely mobile: one announcement we did hear was the priest's pointed request to a section of the audience 'For God and the musicians, please do not smoke.'

In the hope of getting a different assessment of how audiences were responding, I had prepared a simple questionnaire. Two or three questions set out to find out how much Shakespeare was known, and in what language, and whether seen or read: whether the RSC had been attended before, and whether there had been difficulty in following. A more provocative question asked whether the play as seen was thought politically to favour the Left or the Right. A final question asked for further comments. Balbine Huet was happy to arrange with the foyer staff for about a hundred duplicated questionnaires to be put in programmes for the two performances on Sunday. Twenty-one people took trouble to answer. All but two had seen the RSC before, and all those had seen *Henry 5*: many had seen the company in England. All but three knew the play before they came, most, but not all, from reading it in French – they said they were going to study it further. Just over half said in various ways that they found the language of the play difficult to follow. One said '*Je ne comprends pas l'anglais mais j'ai pu apprécier la beauté musicale de cette langue*' and another, charmingly, admitted not to speaking English '*mais à la fin je croyais le parler!*'

My 'political' question provoked some sharp replies. On the whole the feeling was that what they had seen was politically neutral, though five came down on the Right, some with hesitations, and one firmly on the Left. One wrote '*certaine-ment* contre *les deux*'. One pointed out that the play asked questions and thus was a liberal play. Remembering the heavily-slanted adaptations that Europe has seen, I found endearing the answer which said '*Moi et la politique . . . Je ne me suis pas posé la question en assistant à la pièce.*'

All wrote asking for more RSC in Paris, and all powerfully praising, and thanking, the company. Several noted the excellence in the smallest parts: all praised Alan Howard, or said something very appreciative indeed of Charles Dance. Several noted that they were actors themselves, and spoke of learning a great lesson: 'you have shown us what work is, what faith is, what enthusiasm and life are' and one – not an actor – concluded – '*J'ai passé un après-midi de rêve!*' Most concluded '*Bravo et Merci*'.

The bulk of the Paris press notices came after we had left, eleven major comments, by European standards full and rounded in their appreciation. There were some long, fresh accounts. *Le Journal* commented on the extraordinary quality of the audience, a '*silence exceptionelle*': the richness of the play is to be found in its ambiguity. *La Croix* emphasised that the austerity of the set focusses attention on the faces of the actors, who 'declaim' the text, '*mais, après tout, ce non-naturel n'est-il pas précisément "théâtral"?*' *Les Nouvelles Littéraires* with an enormous picture decided that the question fascist or non-fascist was irrelevant in considering this play: in Shakespeare's day all governments were authoritarian. Civil and religi-ous wars were so familiar, and it was quite usual for a general to change sides. It is in the study of character that the interest of this play is to be found, and the character of Coriolanus is complex.

Le Nouvel Observateur said that Howard, like Gielgud, like Olivier, but even more so, is 'the Elizabethan race perpetuated . . . with the same ambiguities, the same wounded pride that one finds in the heroes of Shakespeare.' The play is '*un magnifique cérémonial*', the production, as usual with Hands, '*grand ami de la Comédie-Française*', '*l'exaltation de la virilité.*' *L'Économie* called it 'a dazzling opera, a ballet of light and shadow' a 'sublime black diamond', '*sans doute le plus grand spectacle de la saison*'. Such acclaim, in many other Parisian papers, sounded as well in notices across France, and even in northern Italy.

A NOTE ON THE 'RIOTOUS' 1933/34 PERFORMANCES AT THE
COMÉDIE FRANÇAISE

In some more recent accounts of these events the impression is given that the
version that was played was unusually inflammatory. Wild adaptations of
Coriolanus are nothing new. Nahum Tate's alterations, for example, extant in a
quarto dated 1682, do X-certificate violence to Shakespeare, making the dying
Aufidius attempt to rape the dying Virgilia; a new character, Nigridius, kills
Menenius and then, having 'Mangled, Gnash't, Rack't, Distorted' Young Martius, is himself slain by Volumnia after her long mad scene: the boy dies, with his
father, on his dead mother. This sort of stuff would certainly rouse any audience
to some kind of strong feeling, especially disgust: we are told that the play was a
failure. Knowing the French interest in the link between the Jacobean English
tragic theatre and Corneille, one might expect Piachaud at least to have gone for a
little classical rant, though one hopes no-one would go as far as the decadent Tate.

Piachaud writes that his play is *'traduite librement . . . et adaptée à la scène
française'*. Written in 1929, it is, however, a pedestrianly faithful, rather dull prose
version, the biggest changes being some slight readjustments of the battle-scenes
in Act One and a little playing-down of Aufidius. One has to look very closely to
see anything beyond a general blunting of effect. I suppose the words of the
Tribunes could be said to be slightly expanded at one or two points, and the
People occasionally say a word or two more: their last words in scene 13, 'We will
do so: almost all / Repent in their election' become *'Très bien . . . Il n'aura pas la voix
. . . l'élection n'est pas valable . . . c'est le pire ennemi du peuple . . . À bas Coriolan.'* But
the 'mutable, rank-scented meinie' has become *'cette plèbe immonde, elle qui n'a ni
vergogne ni foi'* and 'You common cry of curs' is *'Vous n'avez pas fini d'aboyer, mauvais
chiens?'* Piachaud sets up expectations in his introduction to the printed text, in
which he discusses the play as a pre-Corneille tragedy, modestly quoting *'le mot
profond et joli de Voltaire, "Malheur aux faiseurs de traductions littérales!"'* But even
Coriolanus' 'treasonable' lines in scene 14, which, from their political effect in
performance one would expect to set the blood tingling, turn out to be duller than
literal. Shakespeare has

> Thou wretch, despite o'erwhelm thee!
> What should the people do with these bald tribunes?
> On whom depending, their obedience fails
> To th'greater bench. In a rebellion,
> When what's not meet, but what must be, was law,
> Then were they chosen. In a better hour,
> Let what is meet be said it must be meet,
> And throw their power i'th'dust.

Piachaud translates

Tais-toi, gredin, et puisses-tu crever un jour de mal honte. Quel besoin peut avoir le peuple de ces tribunes déplumés? C'est pourtant sur eux qu'il s'appuie pour manquer au Sénat romain. Et comment les a-t-on élus, ces drôles? Quand? A la faveur d'une émeute, dans un de ces moments où la nécessité fait loi contre toute justice. Bon, corrigeons cela. Proclamans que ce qui est juste est nécessaire aussi! Et, renversant leur tribunat grotesque, nous rendrons à la boue ce qui est de la boue.

Piachaud's version was mounted with a certain nervousness, after high-level consultations before rehearsals began. But these, according to Éduard Champion in *Le Comédie Française, Années 1933 et 1934* (Paris, 1935) were simply to check the scrupulous accuracy of the rendering of Shakespeare. Several Paris journals, indeed, later took mild issue over the modernisation of some Shakespearean phrases, one suggesting that Piachaud had *'parlementarisé'* the play, with words like *'Sénat' 'motion'*, and *'proposition'*: there was some linguistic discussion.

Modern commentators should bear in mind the massiveness of this production. The cast numbered two hundred and thirty-one people. Ninety-two of these were Citizens, thirty more were Roman soldiers, forty more were Roman Senators. There were ten *'licteurs romains'*, four *'porte-ensigne'*, three *'grand prê-tres'*. Volumnia had ten attendants, there were five children and four *'jeune filles en blanc'*. Modern assumptions of the balance between spectacle and text will not do: we should visualize the same values as Hollywood epic, or an exceptionally expensive *Aïda*.

It was not only Piachaud's *Coriolan* which was felt to be sensitive at the end of 1933. Many other plays in Paris were not even shown. *Ruy Blas*, for example, was not played from 26 November 1933 to 1 August 1934 *'à cause de son apostrophe fameuse "O ministres intègres!"'* True, rumours of a possible government ban circulated during the first performances of *Coriolan*, and there was a reference in the Chamber of Deputies to a declaration of war on *'l'adaptation du fasciste étranger Piachaud'*.

Of the fifty-two performances between the opening on 9 January 1933 and the close on 30 November 1934, almost all were peaceful, and conducted without incident – and not only those (over half the total) after the beginning of March 1934. Even the dozen performances in December 1933 produced little more than what might be called ordinary Shakespearean excitement, with twenty-one curtain calls and public acclaim for the Admministrator of the Comédie and director of the play, Émile Fabre. The focus of attention for the 'riots' has to be on a few performances in January and early February.

There were rumblings in mid-December in the left-wing press, one inflammatory piece seeing Fabre's choice of play as part of a careful fascist softening-up, noting that Alexandre, the great actor leading the play, had played the Caesars many times. Parts of the press still showed similar agitation a year later, with references to *'la traduction-de-guerre-civile du fasciste suisse Piachaud'*. The overwhelming press interest, however, throughout the twelve months, was on the merit of the production, and on Fabre's declared intention to balance the three dominant parts he found, the tragic, the comic and the popular. The significance of the artistic event was related to the historic opening of *Le Mariage de Figaro*.

A sprightly fourth leader in the *Manchester Guardian* for 21 March 1952 drew on the 1934 events in Paris and implied that for many months 'The Royalists, who commonly called the Republic "the slut", cheered Coriolanus' every outburst against that 'common cry of curs' the populace and their 'bald tribunes' whose power should be 'thrown in the dust'. This very short *Guardian* passage has been much used in accounts of the play and its history, but it does appear in several ways to be exaggerated for lively effect. Serious trouble seems only to have begun when on 17 January 1934 a spectator in the balcony tried to whistle up applause, and tumult resulted; the performance was interrupted and the theatre cleared for a short while. Thereafter, the following five performances in January, on 19, 21, 26, 28, and 31, were disrupted by shouts, hoots and even fisticuffs, as Right-wing parties and partisans (*Action Française*, *Croix de Feu* and so on) started to use the play as a virulent attack on the 'corrupt' Chamber of Deputies. Such events have always to be put into the larger context of the organised rise of fascism in Europe in those months, successful in Germany and Italy, almost successful in France. The two peformances of *Coriolan* in February, on the 2nd and 4th, were very much in the shadow of the tensions of those days. The Paris evening papers on the 3rd announced eight major changes by Daladier in senior government posts. Two of those changes were exceptionally inept. The prefect of police, Jean Chiappe, and the head of the Sûreté Général (Scotland Yard, as it were) M. Thomé, had been reported as being scandalously implicated in the shady dealings and subsequent suicide of a financial adventurer called Stavisky; more serious was the widespread belief that the police had instructed their forces to deal gently with the Right in demonstrations, even when faced with extreme and violent behaviour, and be savage to the Left. Daladier, trying to do something and yet not make martyrs, moved Chiappe to the highest administrative post available – Resident-General in Morocco – and, making a clean sweep of the police, moved the elderly Sûreté head as well, to be the Administrator of the Comédie Française. Much has been made of this move, as if so great was the outburst in the theatre that even the Comédie had to be policed by the most senior authority. Dramatic as it is to think of a situation at the National Theatre so bad that Sir Peter Hall has to be replaced by Sir Robert Mark, the truth seems to be that Daladier wanted to move the old policeman somewhere and chose a harmless billet for him, though there were many who saw the move as political revenge.

What is striking, and never stressed in general accounts, is the astonishment and disbelief with which the move was greeted. There has perhaps been exaggeration, since the events, of the strength of the 'riots', for the surprise at the time was universal. Thomé himself at first refused to believe the move. Bewildered,

Fabre demanded reasons, the same day, and was told *'Il n'y en a pas. On a besoin de votre poste . . .'* Outrage and disbelief are paramount in the records. A young Comédie actress said *'Enfin, est-ce qu'ils savent que la Comédie Française est un théâtre?'* Francois Goguel, in *La Politique des Partis sous la 111° Republique*, (Paris, 1946) wrote

la nomination au Théâtre français de l'ancien directeur de la Sûreté donnait au mouvement administratif décidé par Daladier, une allure de vaudeville dont on s'explique mal que ni le président du Conseil ni ses collaborateurs personnels n'aient en conscience. (Tome 11 1933–39, pp. 239–40)

The performance of *Coriolan* that night, 4 February, opened to a packed house with *'un air de bataille'*. A balcony speaker at a brief scene-change stood and spoke for Fabre, and a sensational declaration of support followed from the entire house. The unfortunate Thomé was spotted in a box. Alexandre appealed for calm. At the very end of the play, the iron came down but the audience would not budge, clamouring for Fabre's reinstatement. Alexandre, still in costume, pointed out the danger of a blackout (the theatre was running on safety batteries, as the electricity had earlier failed for a few seconds), and the house cleared. Outside, Fabre found himself facing a massive popular demonstration of support.

All the next day Fabre was the subject of a formidable movement of sympathy and indignation, and on the 6th he was summoned and notified of a new decision: at 5.00 p.m. M. Thomé was relieved of the post he had never occupied, and Fabre reinstated. But Paris was then occupied with the heavy fighting which made that day so famous, and all theatres were closed for several days. The Comédie reopened on the 9th with *Les Précieuses Ridicules* and *Le Malade Imaginaire*. A newspaper headline on the 12th had *'Acré, Shakespeare, v'la les flics!'* and the next day one observed, *Coriolan en exil . . .!* The play returned normally on 11 March.

What is striking in that piece of theatre-history is neither the fascist intrusion nor the anti-fascist rhetoric, but the overwhelming energy demonstrated by audiences in favour of Shakespeare produced as well as was thought possible. 'A plague', those Fabre-supporters are clearly saying, 'on both your political houses.'

Four

Vienna

On the urban motorway to Charles de Gaulle airport, the other RSC coach, on a different lane, overtook us. 'Oh, look'!, said one of the company, with exaggerated, pretended, awe, *'there's the Royal Shakespeare Company!'* That slightly surreal moment made a model for the next seventy-two hours. After an unexpectedly pleasant lunch, with good wine, over the alps in an Air France Caravelle, at Vienna airport we pushed trolleys past groups of police with sub-machine guns to our coaches, in warm sunshine.

I met John Moore in one of the wide high corridors backstage at the Burgtheater: like a slow White Rabbit, he muttered as he passed me, 'It's all a dream, it's all a dream. Please say it's all a dream.' That gracious, spacious, theatre was, backstage, full of problems. The lorries, had not, after all, made Vienna in time: a faulty headlamp had caused them to be refused clearance at one of the frontiers, where they lost four hours. So Terry, who had been there in advance, organised the bringing out of store of his old *Troilus* stage, with gantries longer and much higher than the *Coriolanus* ones; and the stage-floor was covered with black cloth and, within an hour, imitation boards were superbly painted on by the Burg staff. The lorries later disgorged their walls and lanterns and props and skips near an already-built basic set. The 'wrong' gantries meant that the musicians, and the follow-spot operators, and, in this theatre, Di, were going to have to do vertical climbs to unusually high perches in the dark; and the actors were going to have difficult entrances and exits up and down steps, and even slightly round corners.

The backstage facilities and administrative areas of the Burg are in two opposing sections, which a mere scribe found maddeningly difficult, since they are identical. They were not, however, to be confused by anybody else, on pain of tight-lipped Viennese hostility everywhere, for one was a male wing and one was a female wing and never the twain should meet according to the laws of the Burgtheater. Lucy, for example, trying to get on quietly with Alan first and then all the rest as usual, in careful, relaxed sequence, found herself shadowed when she had to appear at the door of a male dressing-room. Males had male dressers, females had female dressers, and there was severe disapproval of the lax RSC ways of bother-less interchange, a few key staff doing everybody. Lucy, again,

A staircase in the Burgtheater.

found that her job was normally done at that theatre by seventeen people.

Something, a sort of psychic virus, got into the entire company. Alan was still ill, and not sleeping. Graham and others were far from well. Terry, with us for some of the days, was also in demand at Covent Garden. Ian Judge, who had previously worked on the play as Assistant Director, came for twenty-four hours to help. Alistair and others felt that technically the RSC looked shabby. Though it was universally agreed that the unsmiling Viennese stage-technicians were amazingly good, like a superbly-drilled army, there was also much discomfort with them; they thought they had understood English explanations of what they had to do when in fact they hadn't. There was one interpreter, when at least four were needed. There was no possibility of verbal communication from Di to anywhere, during the show. It seemed to everyone that rules and regulations, not necessarily matching the work of the theatre, governed everything – the outward signs of an official system coming from somewhere else. Thus, when I first walked from the back corridor on to the stage amid the chaos of getting-in and building and attempted focussing, I first of all met not the close, comforting, womb-like darkness of the Odéon, but wide light expanses of stage with our set sitting on the front edge like a small exotic caged animal – and near it a group of formal Viennese in hats standing round a guide. Backstage at the Burg is one of the Sights of Vienna, it seems; while Mike Taylor was working on the lighting-plot, calling for single lamps in the darkness, his work was suddenly made impossible as all the house-lights came up; a party came round the theatre and was lectured to before the house-lights went down again. But front of house – ah, what glory! When had any of the actors in this company played in so grand a theatre? The foyers in their magnificence beggar description, and the RSC office, with Hal lost in a far corner, was a room worth a visit for its own sake, reducing anyone who went in to proper human size in such soaring elegance.

There I first talked to Sue Whitmarsh, travelling teacher to the Young Martiuses, who is very used to working in bizarre places having once, on film location, taught for three days down a manhole, and done maths astride a three-thousand volt cable. The cheerful competence of these two boys owed much to Sue, who had decided that it would be folly to do The Amoeba when every minute of the trip, every eye-blink, was a lesson in geography, history, economics, international affairs, transport and comparative culture. So the boys learned about what was around them, and made illustrated journals of the trip. In almost equally grand surroundings in Vienna I interviewed Jan de Blick, the European impresario handling the tour, a benign Dutch business-man with the past, present and future cultural life of Europe at his finger-tips. From him, and from Bill Wilkinson later, I heard the reasons why attempts to take the production behind the Iron Curtain had not been successful. Because it is impossible for a British company to take money out of either Warsaw or Prague, the two cities first tentatively included in the planning, arrangements have to be made with the British

The RSC office in the Burgtheater, the DSM (Diane West) and the Stage Manager (Philip Hoare) at work.

Government through the British Council, and diplomatically sensitive and subtle deals have to be arranged with the national governments. Both the Poles and the Czechs were anxious to have this play: the British Council was enthusiastic about the RSC visiting those countries. The Council said, however, that the suggested dates were not suitable, and the funds available in those countries for companies such as the RSC had already been fully used for that year. Eventually, a contract with Warsaw did come through, the result of intensive beavering-away by the British international-theatre impresario Molly Daubeny, on the RSC's behalf: but it came too late, and for dates already committed to Zürich, and therefore, as Bill Wilkinson said, 'the question of available financial resources to support such a visit was never investigated.' Though the RSC pressed, hard, for a long time, they had in the end to accept that it was impossible. It was a pity, for that production of that play above all should have been seen in Eastern Europe. Here we were in Vienna, with road-signs pointing to Prague, but having instead to come all the way back to England for eight days.

A fight-rehearsal at the Burg. Alan asks into the auditorium darkness, 'Will some-one tell me what is happening?' From the stalls Ian Judge replies, apologising; they have a lighting problem and had not known it was half past four. They will take the scene now. Lights change. Alan and Charlie begin. Alan stops. 'What the hell are these doing here?' Tempers are rising. I think the 'these' might be people, perhaps Viennese in hats, and tremble for them. But they are tight circles of light on the stage. 'Terry wanted them', someone says. 'Well take them out, they're in the way' says Alan crossly. There is a moment of pause, of tension, of commands in Viennese German into the void. All the stage lights go out. Alan groans. The lights come back, different, but still wrong. Philip stands on stage and calls out a number. Austrian mutterings from the stalls, into a mike. Alan and Charlie rest, stooped over their sharp swords on the floor. Nothing happens. The lights change again, twice. A patient feminine voice from the side (Di's) explains precisely what is wanted. Mixed muttering from the stalls; more Viennese shouting of commands. Alan slowly stands up and mimes cutting off his head with both swords locked at his neck like scissors. The lights come back, right, and the fight begins, slow and cool: but loss of temper, like a thunder-cloud, hangs around. The storm breaks, again over lighting, and Alan in mid-stroke strides off stage. 'What about me?' asks Charlie.

I have met and had long talks with Dr Erika Zabrsa, bird-like and with voluble English, who runs the Burgtheater press-office. She is extremely helpful, and makes elaborate arrangements for me to have a seat in the house that night. I have to stand at point X in the wonderful lower foyer, and be met by Herr Y, who will personally conduct me, all ticket-less as I am, to Herr Z at one side of the stalls, who will put me on a little flap-seat in an exit-corridor.

Later, though I am as tidily-dressed as I can be, I feel scruffy in this big formal house: twelve hundred people, most, it seems, in full evening-dress. There is much discreet waving, and men make little bows across the four ranks of boxes. The only eye I catch is Jan de Blick's, in a box opposite me.

Though the house coughs and is inattentive and even sleepy, the performance is excellent. I had never seen the choreography of the groups so admirable, their sudden rushings and sudden freezings, black frescoes picked out with silver and gold. As the huge gates of Corioles swing, I see through to Alistair and a crouched, pushing group of stage-hands: a lamp has been left up on the whole up-stage area. As the gates open, showing Alan at the top, and close again, Alistair is brilliantly there too, careful and watching.

A bad misunderstanding began act two, a literally glaring mistake, and virtu-ally the only one of the tour. The iron went up far too early – something quite out of Di's control – and with no signal given, the stage lights came up, the house lights suddenly went out, and the audience instantly hushed. But nothing hap-pened, of course, for Graham, who begins the act alone, was far away. The Burg technicians had taken it on themselves to cut that interval to two minutes. The audience giggled in the darkness, and began a slow hand-clap as the minutes went by and nothing whatsoever happened on the empty stage. Good-nature stopped the hand-clap, and after a long and deeply embarrassed silence from twelve-hundred and one persons, Graham strolled calmly on.

That night, out at Grinzing at the reception in honour of the RSC so generously given by the Burgtheater, everyone was to have what our Viennese hosts did tend, unfortunately, to describe to us as A Jolly Evening. On that occasion, I believe, the informality of the English led to some misunderstanding, as actors – and certainly actresses – did not usually, in Austrian experience, talk to Viennese technicians. I was fortunate to sit with Angela Zabrsa, Erika's sister, herself an Assistant Director who had worked with Terry, and Rudolf Weys who had translated the *Troilus and Cressida* which Terry had produced; they explained their fascination with what they called the English classical acting style and its musical freedom. I was struck by this use of 'classical' meaning almost 'sanctioned histori-cally' for something rich, flowing, and emotional in so 'classical' a city, where ponderous largeness, a straining formality, and rigid differentiation of social rôles – and even gender rôles – pointed to the opposite of what I felt were the flexibilities of voice and gesture in Alan and the rest.

Journal. Vienna. Thursday. Awoken very early by Erika phoning: would I do a broadcast interview at nine? When I had got to bed the birds had long been singing in the silent city-centre, so I did not expect to be bright, and indeed I spent a lot of the interview mopping scalding coffee from my trousers. I wonder now what I said. Ian Judge was also there, like me owlishly blinking.

I have now explored a good deal of Vienna, in the course of finding various people to interview. For a city so famously proud of itself the centre is curiously lacking street-maps, public clocks, public loos, a market, even ordinary shops. A meal was shatteringly expensive. Moreover, among the massive blocks of masonry, the huge, solid, unfriendly buildings, it seems to be a grim business, being a Viennese, to my surprise. There are very many grey, sad, elderly people. Perhaps this is one reason why the Company feels so strangely oppressed. An anxious sadness seems to hang in the air, a drooping, silent sorrow on old faces waiting for trams or serving in shops. It is not like the absolute, ultimate, despair I have marked on faces in city subways in America, or in the same country as a look in the eyes of youngish suburban wives bringing children home from school in enormous cars. This is a rather frightened, careful, emotion about the past, not the future. I joined a group going round the Opera (though I didn't stand on the stage in a hat) and I found we often, even there, had to be let through locked doors. Vienna is, I recollect, close to some very uncomfortable frontiers. The weather today is brilliant, and many of the Company seem to have taken themselves into the Vienna Woods: I doubt if there will be dancing.

Terry, we can see, is loved here, not least because he deals with everyone as equals, using Christian names: in a powerfully union-controlled organisation where actors, stage-management and stage-staff are sharply demarcated, that must seem very fine. But soon after he arrived to be with us, it seemed, he was off again to London – twice. From the middle of his opening night of *Parsifal* at Covent Garden he phoned to know how our performance had gone: his return, it turned out, had been delayed, and though he had gone straight from Heathrow to the Opera House, he had missed the first thirty-five minutes. In the second interval he had been able to scramble into a Moss Bros evening-suit-and-black-tie ready for the reception at the end; at which, thus clad, he was scarcely recognised; and after which he flew back to Vienna to be with us.

Erika kindly arranged that my questionnaires should be distributed on the second night. Of the hundred and seventeen returned, over a third had seen Terry's RSC *Henry 5* with Alan at the Theater an der Wien in Vienna on the previous tour. Seventeen had seen the Berliner Ensemble (Brecht) version at the Burgtheater in 1978. Half had seen one or more RSC productions before, half knew the play before they came, half found difficulty with the language – but among the half who didn't, quite a few native English appeared. My 'political' question received much qualification. Almost everybody found the play political, but most found it impossible to categorize in modern terms – there was a lot of worrying at that particular bone. Forty-six, however, came down firmly on a political side: sixteen found that the play they had seen pointed to the Left, and thirty to the Right.

These documents make a further chorus of admiration, for the level of speaking, for Alan's acting, for the sheer power of the theatrical event: the last question, in particular, inviting further comment, produced a *thesaurus* of Viennese synonyms for 'magnificent', an anthology of enthusiasms. And though several knew the play in Hungarian, and there was one Japanese, the expectation that the audience in Vienna would be the most completely 'native' of the tour seemed to be borne out. This second night in the Burg included a great number of dedicated theatre-goers who had seen a lot of Shakespeare. Their enthusiasm therefore meant much more: and though their answers to my questions seemed at first less critically sophisticated than those later from Hamburg or Munich, the context of their appreciation was in fact wider. One writer noted the 'astonishing courage to go for a naturalistic style, known to me only otherwise in the Russian theatre'; several made good comparisons with the admired 'intensity' of *Henry 5*. Through all the praise for Alan, 'one of the best actors in the world', there was great appreciation of the play as a whole performed by the company as a whole, and discussion of it both as a tragedy and in relation to plays not by Shakespeare. One writer neatly answered the political question with: '"Political" at its best in the sense of Henry Adams: "Politics, as a practice, whatever its professions, has always been the systematic organisation of hatreds."'

The tone of these answers, in essence, is of warm affectionate surprise, like someone getting to know for the first time young, distant members of the family and finding them both brilliant and unexpectedly friendly. Many writers stressed Hands' excellence especially in that he does not violate Shakespeare. 'It is, however', wrote one, 'to be noticed that Hands has got actors who are above any middle-European level. As an enthusiastic theatre-goer in Vienna ever since my childhood I confess this grievingly (*muss ich das schweren Herzens zugeben*)'. In a city which has so dominated the cultural experience of Europe there is still much important occupation with matters of plays and players. Indeed, I felt I detected some desperation, even, in that interest; an older generation holding on to evidences of a once-predominant social and cultural glory.

So the Viennese press gave us the longest notices of the tour: in five papers alone a total of three and a half thousand words. The *Neue Kronen-Zeitung* began with a trumpet-call, 'A roar of applause after four hours of Shakespeare!' The *Weiner Zeitung* said 'Most productions of *Coriolanus* don't know how to cope with the play. They either "support" the text by means of some ideological interpretation, like Brecht, or they flounder in pompous historicism, dwelling on ritualised battle-scenes and portraying Romans and plebs in the manner of school Latin books. Not so Terry Hands. He lets the text, and only the text, have its say.'

Neue Kronenzeitung again: 'Hands' *Coriolanus* is a gripping, robust piece of theatre. Dark, gloomy, his staging gains its effect from its bald directness. A loud, harshly contoured, angular Shakespeare this, without obscuring the fine structure of the play.' Caius Martius is 'an egoist, thirsting to do deeds, with a piercing glance and cutting voice.' *Wochenpresse*: 'It was made clear in a wonderful way how unbroken, how untouched by intellectual doubt the relationship of the British to their great classic master remains. How, where the poet has written arias in speech, they let them be heard as arias without inhibition . . . The whole of a large ensemble, cast with exactness right down to the tiniest part . . . with what perfection every single performer without exception knows how to speak! . . .

Waiting to leave Vienna. Left to right: Sue Whitmarsh, Cynthia Gilman, Paul Imbusch, Charles Dance, Graham Crowden, Ken McClellan.

[There are] perfectly choreographed, beautifully lit duels. Hands keeps the stage free of people and soldiers standing around doing nothing. The People look like a crowd of cheeky little Cockneys and they talk like them . . . Alan Howard . . . lets nothing superfluous creep into this gigantic role'. *Kurier* found in much of the production 'a parodic undertone': '*Pathos* and wit, lament and joke are brought into harmony' – it admirably likened Menenius to 'a Latin G.B. Shaw.'

From the Journal of Paul Basson (Young Martius) aged 9. Tomorrow we fly home for Easter. I am looking forward to going home because I have missed Mum and Dad and the television. I will tell them all about it and what happened.

The air-traffic controllers' go-slow delayed take-off from Vienna for several hours: in spite of that, at the airport enormous effervescence of spirits rose through the whole company: the worst, it suddenly seemed, was over. When we landed at Heathrow, England was green and warm and welcoming and felt, unmistakeably, a land of freedom.

Five

Amsterdam and Brussels

Journal. Saturday 21 April. After the break, I rejoined the company two days late. Coming in to Amsterdam in the late afternoon from the North in a KLM DC 9 over the tidy, watery suburbs was no preparation for traffic jams and confusion, or the depression of arrival at the Hotel Cordial: the statement that I would please wait in the bar, as the gentleman had not finished with my room, sounded sinister. The 'room' when I got up to it (for which I was charged £21.00 for one night) was a small narrow box with a tiny bed, a curtainless echoing shower-space in one corner. Just over twenty-four hours before, I'd been with my family in farthest Cornwall: now I didn't belong anywhere at all.

The lorries had arrived from Vienna on Tuesday. The stage-crew flew in from England on Wednesday. The company had followed on Thursday, a little grumpily because everyone – even those already in Amsterdam – had had to go back to London for the group tickets. For many, leaving a domestic holiday to take up theatrical touring abroad again seemed pretty unacceptable. Mike Hall put it that so much depends on the hotel: if it's cold and bleak, you haven't a snug to retreat to and you can't walk *all* day. There was soft but insistent complaint all the time in Amsterdam about the hotels, and even confusion about who was where. At the theatre the get-in was slow, as everything had to be handled three times, coming off the lorries to be packed into a lift: but at the top there was a big dock (loading-area) giving plenty of room to sort, so the set itself went up quickly. Wrong information about voltage and lamp-settings hindered Basher's lighting, which was therefore extremely slow. The lighting-board worked on a punched-card system which made adjustment of cue-speeds and other corrections slow. John Moore had to re-wire most of the cue lights, and oil for the smoke-gun had spilled into everything in one skip, including an amplifier. The theatre-staff, however, were cheerful and English-speaking – unlike some of the actors, who were miserably unwell, and Bernard's 'I shall lack voice' in scene 12 was unusually prophetic in the first performance.

The audience for that first night was quick and easily-amused. The Staddsschouwburg is one of Holland's historic theatres, with a loyal following. Perhaps that explains the absolute lack of interest shown by the front-of-house staff there. Though I asked Hal several times, he was never able to connect me with any sort of press office: my letter on RSC notepaper asking for copies of press-notices received not even an acknowledgement. There was one poster, somewhere out front. The company was not therefore surprised to find a lot of empty seats.

Those Amsterdamers who were there laughed readily. One delighted burst of laughter and applause came in a least-expected place in scene 23. John Moore, hearing this back-stage, guessed with memories of a famous night at the Aldwych either that one of the theatre-cats had wandered on stage, or that a follow-spot had gone wild. At a crucial moment for Charlie, a Dutch operator had found he couldn't swing his spot. Instead of easing it, he jerked it loose, and the light swung all over the stage as he wrestled with it, finally settling on Charlie on the words 'All places yields to him ere he sits down'. The unlucky operator went straight back-stage at the end of the show and apologized personally. The chief electrician, by contrast, tended to abandon his board during the show in pursuit of Di – and she was having trouble enough with the fire-officers, two young men in an alcoholic haze, one of whom kept leaning over trying to turn the pages for her. The atmosphere could be described as relaxed.

There was no official reception, and no welcome of any kind. This was explained as the result of the Embassy being in mourning for the political murder of the British Ambassador in The Hague exactly a month before. This appalling event, however, cannot really explain the many empty seats at the back of the stalls. Company morale needed lifting. A bright warm day would have helped, and so would a little local notice. I tended to come across members of this young and lively Company muttering in bolshie mood. Of course there never was a troupe of actors *not* at odds with the management, even if that management were a Company. Of course too, actors on tour are sensitive: minor hiccups become major upsets – for a few minutes. Feelings swing about like Dutch follow-spots. I was always aware of two, to me, extraordinary effects. The first was how unlike actors are to academics: in my world, across the globe, grudges can be nurtured, sometimes for whole professional lifetimes: among these actors, they were forgotten in two hours. And whatever happened, the performance varied only between the outstanding and the inspired: the permitted tolerance was about half of one per cent less than perfection. Yet the company was unhappy in Amsterdam. Rumours of all kinds spread quickly: it was said that Terry was not after all coming to Brussels.

The Saturday house was a little fuller, but otherwise much the same. The most informal audience we had on the tour, by far, the strongest element in it clearly wanted entertainment. In American parlance we were 'a show'. So there were ripples of laughter throughout Graham's first scene with the citizens – they loved the shooting-stick – but dead silence on Ruth's classical joke about Penelope. It was good to have smoke again in the battle-scenes, and the echo-effects in the splendid acoustics sounded very grand. Alan's vicious 'Hang 'em'! got a happy laugh from that shallow audience. What was lacking was any sense of occasion

The start of the Pleading scene. Coriolanus (Alan Howard), Aufidius (Charles Dance), Virgilia (Jill Baker), Volumnia (Maxine Audley), Valeria (Ruth Rosen).

whatsoever. It might have been *No Sex Please We're British*: it happened to be Shakespeare. I had no feeling of being present at a significant piece of theatre, least of all at a major tragedy. At the end, many of the audience rose to their feet at once, in the American manner. One person in the stalls near me caused much consternation by shouting 'Hoo, hoo!' vociferously. Several actors taking the curtain-calls pardonably mistook the sound for 'Boo!' and were disconcerted.

I was invited to help with the get-out, and I felt like a small boy allowed to help Daddy. A swarm of cheerful, sweaty young Dutch settled on everything and began to unscrew it, not always wisely. I felt ridiculously pleased when asked by Philip to do a simple job like untying things sent down by rope from the gantries. I admired the way Neil, Philip and Johnny, themselves working very hard, tactfully controlled the over-enthusiastic student casuals and got everything on the trolleys and to the lift in the right order for packing on the lorries – where more student casuals, over-apt to do it their way, in fact tended to hold the process up. The get-out was successfully completed just after four o'clock. At half past two I left with Hal and Di, walking in pouring rain back to the hotel through a city still active and brilliantly lit.

Journal. 2.0 p.m. Sunday. Over a strange breakfast – should one really sprinkle hundreds-of-thousands over liver-sausage? – Ken McClellan told me about the inside of a windmill he'd been in yesterday, now a paint mill, and only one of seventeen left out of four hundred. At half-past ten I walked in quiet streets by canals amid seventeenth-century buildings, listening to church-bells like musical-boxes, passing the open door of a Salvation Army service almost next – as it should be – to the girls in the windows, at their positions even at this godly hour. Now on the coach to Brussels, two of the sick men of Europe, Graham and Bernard, are looking better: Bernard is telling splendid stories of working with Robert Atkins: Atkins, old and deaf, playing Falstaff to a young Pistol he disliked, greeted Pistol's entry, and the news that the old King is dead and their Hal now king, with 'Oh, bugger that old son, do go away.'

When I did see Press notices from Amsterdam, a very long time after the tour, I found them full of high astounding terms, lavish in their praise, and contradictory about detail: one said that 'the lighting is focused almost entirely on the glorifica-tion of the main character', another linked the lighting with the group-movements. One lamented that the 'monstrous *Übermensch*' . . . 'the temptation of the fascist ideal', is 'anything but a tragic character': another (two days later) more sensitively pointed to many elements, anxious to maintain 'the philosophi-cal impartiality of the play's creator', saying of the hero that 'his righteousness and his incorruptibility . . .' makes the play 'all the more tragic'. Several praise the whole ensemble. All the Dutch notices I have seen are struck by the lighting and the set, and by Alan, who is 'worthy to take over from Laurence Olivier', and almost 'speaks polyphonically'. The *Handelsblad* critic concludes 'It is an astound-ing performance which knocks me about to a degree. So astounding that I seem hardly able to think. Whether this is the effect it should have I venture to doubt.'

The company snatched odd food at a windy, rainy and meaningless frontier-post: currency, language, habits and customs all changed invisibly. The Palace Hotel in Brussels was by contrast with Amsterdam . . . well, palatial, in the old style, everything huge and wide and high and carpeted. There was probably a Palm Court with an orchestra, though I never found it.

The theatre was less than a minute away. And that, most people said, was about the best that could be said for a place I can only describe as a National Theatre, Woolworth's style. It occupied part of several floors in an ugly twenty-eight-storey office-block. Inside, the lack of back-stage accommodation was caus-ing something beyond gloom: during performances, it was impossible to go, backstage, from one side of stage to another except by going through the wings of a smaller theatre alongside: care had to be taken not to tangle with the very different social-comment drama running on the smaller stage at the same time. I realised I would find that more of a problem than the RSC company did: I was always surprised by the extra perceptions the actors and crew seemed to have. They would dump a case in a hotel room and go straight to the theatre, to look at the stage and the dressing-rooms, and they would do easily all the things that I found hard, like discovering the stage-door and sorting out strange levels and corridors, to say nothing of getting to know instantly the local staff. In the eight

Théâtre National, Brussels.

very different theatres we played at, it was I who got lost and scurried past the same row of unmarked identical doors six times like a mouse in a maze.

The new Théâtre National building in Brussels, that is to say the French-speaking half of the Belgian National Theatre, is seventeen years old: in 1978 it was closed for three months and was entirely re-furbished, with a new auditorium. Much new equipment is still in the process of being installed – a new English sound-desk, for example. The lighting-board was still not good, being half new and half old. The auditorium, with its ceiling starred with naked light-bulbs, was, like the whole complex, of unhappy design: and the two days in that theatre were for most of the company not a memory to cherish. Many of the technical staff were going on tour themselves the day after our first performance. The now-customary problem of wrong information was exacerbated – certain essential items such as dressing-rooms were just not there. Di had to put the seven Citizens, the thirteen strong Band, the Stage-Management and Props all in one rehearsal room, where there were no mirrors, lights or basins. (Though the company had been told before leaving England, in March, that every theatre had good washing facilities except one, all over Europe costumes were being taken home at night by local back-stage staff to be washed and pressed in distant suburbs.)

I was fortunate. The Théâtre National has an excellent archive, on the premises, run, and largely created by, a true theatre-scholar, the young Danielle De

Boeck, herself very knowledgeable about English theatre, and an accomplished translator. She put the files at my disposal. There I first saw, rising like a giant moon, on the cover of a souvenir booklet, the extraordinary bald wig in which Boy Gobert of the Thalia-Theater in Hamburg played Coriolanus in the version that company brought to this theatre in 1977. In this souvenir-programme I first saw stressed that idea which so dominates German adaptations of the play that I have studied – that in the class-war between patricians and plebs which *Coriolanus* is said to expound, the only weapons the plebs have is the refusal of military service. This matter was apparently made quite central in the Thalia presentation. (There have been many adaptations of this play in Europe; I refer only in this book to those which in some way impinged on the Company and the tour in 1979.)

The actors were called for half-past four on Monday, and the act one run-through was relaxed; Alan was amused at his micro-second delay giving 'Come I too late?' an extra force. At one point he stood centre-stage and said 'Are you happy with this change?' apparently to his feet. It was Hands who replied, from the darkness of the stalls, and understood the reference to slightly altered lighting. At a run-through like this, the actors wear head-gear to help the follow-spot operators identify the figures they are following, so I watched from the stalls an army in jeans, woolly-jumpers and Roman helmets. Terry spoke softly to the company on stage at the end, giving notes on technical matters of detail, anxious for them all to get rest. The actors left, and lighting continued, Alistair standing-in for Alan on the walls. A young Belgian technician on his way up to one of the lanterns seemed to me to be simply climbing like a fly straight up the side of the auditorium.

The big walls opened, and the stage was swept methodically by Alistair and the Brussels stage-hands, including two girls – all casual workers, students who were new to the theatre. The Chief Electrician in his blue coat stood with a head-set, talking to invisible operators. The musicians on their gantries tootled while, mike by mike, their sound was balanced, Gordon Kember and John Moore meeting on stage after each adjustment. With David Hissey above conducting the full music of cue 52, the hero's final entrance, the Belgian crew practised moving the four walls. The stage was full of people; least conspicuous was Terry talking to Basher. I realized how familiar it had become to watch people walk down stage and, peering into the darkness, call out in several languages. The stage, from the back, was mopped down, driving everyone forward until eighteen people stood in a row, looking upstage, on the narrow apron, absorbed in their own work. With Jacqui, the red-headed interpreter familiar from Paris, Basher and Di spoke out, in two languages, with a third in use, the sequence of cues for stage-lights and house-lights or curtain-calls. Almost everyone left. Terry, talking also with Di, clutching phones to his ears, muttered rapid French into his headset: after intervals of some time, lights changed. The stage was suddenly plunged into total darkness, to satisfied 'aahs' all round. It was six-twenty.

Back-stage discussion during a get-out: the DSM (Diane West), Stage Manager
(Philip Hoare), Chief Stage Technician (Neil Robson).

I hauled Terry off for tea and sandwiches amid the gilt and mirrors of the Palace
Hotel. We had a lot of talk to catch up, including all the strong feelings surrounding his Covent Garden *Parsifal*, and experiences on this tour so far. He quoted
Alistair saying that the senior stage technicians in Vienna were amazed that every
single member of the RSC crew did the work of three of them, except for Di who
did the work of four.

At that evening's performance, Terry did his usual trick of effortlessly, and
almost invisibly, spending most of his time talking to the actors in their dressing-
rooms, also spending most of his time seeing the show from out front, and also
spending most of his time adjusting lighting-states from the box. In spite of
immense difficulties, Philip being convinced right up until the signal to go that
there would be a terrible mess, the performance was technically very good,
though there had not been time to get lighting perfect. The actors were on top
form, playing easily and very well, though the audience-response was dull and
low. Obvious points were solidly taken, like Alan's "Mildly" at the end of scene 15
which got a round of applause. The house, seating 850, was far from full.

In the interval I took myself into the crowd. Two English girls came near me,
one saying cattishly to the other 'Oh, I *do* think the RSC are *terribly* hamming it
up', and saying that a recent RSC *Much Ado* was 'disgusting'. Not fans, I gathered.
Two Belgian girls speaking only French were thoughtfully impressed, and strug-
gled to clarify answers to my questions. They followed easily, they said, and
found the 'English style' so grand and so open and so full, so unlike their own
style. They had seen no other RSC plays, and were bowled over. What surprised
and delighted them was the sense of completion right through, to the meanest

part. I spoke to them again at the end: they gave as an example of their surprise and delight David Shaw-Parker's 'poor gentleman' passage: such a small part was so full and so rounded: the whole experience was so tremendous, as they put it, right down to the very bottom of the casting.

After the performance, we were taken by coach to an official reception at the British Embassy. Sir Peter and Lady Wakefield received us in their beautiful residence. Politely, but very hungrily, the fifty-six RSC people fell on the food, apparently endlessly supplied on the mahogany table under the crystal chandelier. I was introduced to Ros Falvey, the British Council representative, who told me later how impressed she had been at that reception by the cheerful friendliness of everyone from the RSC, and that there had been no 'side'. She, experienced in these matters, had for once not been able to tell the difference between technicians and actors, 'unlike . . .' she said musingly, but could not be persuaded to break that diplomatic discretion. She had watched, she said, Alan listening with total attention to a French lady giving her views on Shakespeare, Alan throughout the model of extreme courtesy and patience. Graham had been equally patient, though he confessed privately to boredom, stuck with a long account from someone who explained how silly she was, but she did have this odd notion, which suddenly came to her during the performance, that some of Shakespeare might just, by somebody perhaps, be considered a tiny bit relevant, I mean, to *today*?

I thought at first he had been unlucky. Yet most of us, wandering through those wonderful rooms, the pink and the blue and the yellow, magnificent food and drink in hand, found social difficulties, and ended up talking shop together. Few of the guests made an effort to speak to us (I suppose they had waited a long time for us to arrive), and when they did, it turned out that few had seen the show, and fewer still had enjoyed it at all; they tried to get us to agree what a dreary play it was. Philip reported a very senior diplomat confiding in him what a bloody awful play he had found it – he didn't follow some of it at all. 'One just sat there and let it wash over you much of the time. I suspect that some of you chaps were doing the same'. All this turned Graham a little maverick, and he wandered from room to room saying from side to side 'How *very* kind of you, how do you do, how *very* kind of you', and then kissed Lady Wakefield good-night as he left. Deirdra, talking with a tall distinguished man, heard a reference to 'this English company'. 'Actually,' she said, 'I'm Irish – but don't tell the Ambassador.' 'I am the Ambassador,' said the Ambassador.

Maxine had secretly organized the warmest part of the occasion: standing at the far end of the table in the dining room, she most imperiously commanded silence (Volumnia now with more than a touch of Ftatateeta) and, being Maxine, got it instantly. She then made a little speech about it being Shakespeare's birthday, and he being four hundred and fourteen. But much more importantly, she said, it is also the birthday of Paul Basson (one Young Martius) who is ten today. Paul, called to come through the press of people, looked very pleased indeed, and went and stood with Maxine, and found himself facing a cake with ten candles, which he blew out in one puff while we sang 'Happy Birthday'.

Everyone agreed, going home, that the food had been wonderful. Terry stood in the coach and said that it had been a good show that night, crisp, alert, live and rapid. He said that they would find Hamburg full of actors for a big theatre-festival, so they should keep it crisp and light and fast.

From the journal of Stephen Humphries, (Young Martius) aged 11. . . . After the play had finished I got ready for the reception. At the reception as soon as you walked in you were given a plate for some food. The food was not very nice, but I ate the pudding. The house we went to was massive and it belonged to Lord and Lady Wakefield. The house had a lot of rooms which were very big. I enjoyed the party very much.

Next day Danielle told me that several of their Théâtre National players had seen the show the night before and had been overwhelmed. They felt that after that they couldn't continue, it was so perfect and so wonderful – they couldn't go on with what they were doing. She, herself, like so many in Europe, commented first of all on the more open, more dramatic style. Their own actors were afraid of what Shakespeare has said – they don't go up to the end of the feeling, but stop in the middle as she put it. She had not seen a Belgian Shakespeare that pleased her, and blamed the French language, as being more flat, not so possible to use as a musical instrument. She spoke of the many changes the German version from the Thalia-theater in Hamburg had made, and how in that production some people in the smaller rôles were not good. In any case, she said with a little impatience, the play is much more than politics; it is more about power, and power is more than politics.

I was told by several of the company of the speed with which Alan learned the part, and how rapidly he developed the extraordinary range of voice and effect which he used. Alan himself told me that he had made sure he knew most of the play before rehearsals started. (People often described him to me as a 'rhetorical' actor: the epithet might well fit his Hal or Henry 5, or passages of his Henry 6, and certainly much of his Coriolanus, though it should not suggest that other approaches are outside his range.)

Alan said, about the language of the play, 'It is very very precise, especially in its use of conjunctions and prepositions, legally precise in fact, in order to tie down exactly what people are trying to say, or rather trying not to say. Yet at the same time, by clever use of such parts of speech, he can evade the truth, produce an effect which is apparently arranged to be absolutely precise, but it is at the same time slightly off. So the very spare language combines a poetical ambiguity with extraordinary directness. It is accurate at the time it is uttered, but then the circumstances rapidly alter and everything shifts. We found it a very deceptive play in its denseness. We'd all be sitting around in the early stages, and our first reading would be political, and a page later we'd start questioning everything

Mother and son; Volumnia (Maxine Audley) and Coriolanus (Alan Howard).

we'd just decided. People were finding themselves quite retracting their first positions. Shakespeare does seem to present alternative arguments when he's supposed to be on the Left or the Right – its not as easy as that. It is a play intensely about the people in it. And Coriolanus, when he wants to, can speak with astonishing intellectual power and passion, something he combines in the 'corn-debate' in scene 14, where its almost as if he has been given the gift of tongues.

The musicians were always an essential part of the RSC on tour; not only in their personal contribution to general well-being, but very properly representing the Company's musical achievements in European centres. In Brussels, the Brass Quintet gave a lunchtime concert for the European Commission. They played in the EEC building in a conference room of padded walls, translation-booths and long tables, decorated in discreet greens, browns and greys like a grown-up schoolroom. Unlike the over-live acoustics of the Church of St Merri in Paris, here the effect was dry; but in the crowded room, with many people sitting on tables, those fine brass sounds came across very well, and the programme was much enjoyed, the Poulenc and Walton pieces in particular causing smiles and ripples of laughter. The Quintet, in their working blacks, looked like five young Hamlets in a drawing-room; they were five smiling, bowing Hamlets after the exhilarating final Scheidt fugue, which everyone went out happily humming.

Journal. Brussels. 5.30. Tuesday. I take my paranoia for a walk, having disguised it from myself for long enough. This company is young, happy, lively and very friendly: I am quite remarkably accepted everywhere. But I am *not* a member. I am always an outsider, observing, noting. In a group like this there are sensitivities, irritations, a network of feelings, and at times I feel many of these pointing at me in a way that is hard to take. I visit St Nicholas' Church, fine and interesting Romanesque, some of it a thousand years old. I look at the ikon done in Constantinople in 1115, and taken to Kiev. My problems seem a little smaller. In the Grande Place I stand in front of the house where Victor Hugo lived, lucky chap, in 1852, and realise that paranoia is the occupational disease of academics as well as writers, and I am both. But I do think that I have deceived myself. I thought I was invisible, because irrelevant, not in any way central to the matter, and therefore easy to ignore. But I fear I have been all too significant, a spy. Of course, unlike every other member of the Company, my work is invisible. All the activity of the theatre is towards instant display. But I go round – sometimes, I fear, it must seem that I creep around – watching. They must wonder, some of them, what I'm up to, with a way of life clearly worse than just peculiar in its very hiddenness. There is nothing whatsoever to show for it – yet. But in black ink my love may still shine bright, though it is unlikely to last as long as the ikon from Kiev.

I walk on and presently stare at the Mannikin Pis, so much tinier than I expected. And there, I tell myself, is a lesson for us all. I walk back to the hotel feeling better.

There are fifteen thousand English-speaking people in Brussels, and Ros Falvey reckons that for a show like ours we can count on half an audience being English-speaking. Our second night's performance was as good as the first. The audience was much more alive and alert, with a stillness not of incomprehension or boredom, I felt, but of hungry attention. Perhaps last night we had a minor version of the Vienna Effect, with rows of seats occupied by people largely there for social reasons. My impression on the second night was of an audience unfamiliar with, and thirsting for, largeness of theatrical experience.

Only two of my questionnaires came back to the ark, each with a meagre leaf, and both sharply rebuking me for my 'political' question. The press, however, was fulsome, if not particularly profound: *Le Dernière Heure* pointed out that although the language was difficult, the production enabled the audience to 'read' the action, such was the '*lisibilité*'. *Le Soire* commented on the restraint of staging and costumes in colour and style, the 'relative austerity' of the visual side making an incentive to listen to 'Le texte avant toute chose', and in their service of the dramatic reflections in the play the actors are without equal in the world. Alan Howard is '*prodigieux*': *La Dernière Heure* says '*Il ne joue pas Coriolan, il est Coriolan*': *La Cité* discusses the political and psychological make-up of the character, and gives high praise for other leading actors in the Company. Here in the RSC exists '*une fusion remarquable – qui n'est pas un compromis – de la tradition, et de la modernité*'. 'What a lesson for those who pull the theatre apart in the name of a pseudo-modernity, as aggressive as it is aberrant'. *Le Soir* said '*Oui, messieurs les anglais, vous restez les premiers . . .*'

Six

Hamburg

In the wide spaces of Schiphol's departure-lounges the company, now exactly half-way through the tour, flopped. Everyone sat wearily looking forward to Hamburg. There were to be no calls at all for the first day there, Thursday, so that from arrival on that mid-afternoon, Wednesday, until the rehearsals in the hours before the first performance on Friday there was space. Everyone agreed that the last three places – all two-night stands – had been killing. There was a strong feeling of never having settled down, *ever* – or not at least since Paris, months and months ago, it seemed. A clear day in Hamburg, in a Festival atmosphere, would set everyone up very positively: and to spend five whole days in one city felt like luxury.

The Finnair flight was announced for Helsinki; it was a small touch of the exotic to sit in the tidy, and almost empty, DC9, and be addressed by the cabin staff in Finnish. High over the Iselmeer we flew among peaks and castles of dazzling, towering, white clouds, the insect arrow-heads of shipping far below. Behind me, Ron Cook exclaimed in wonder. However often you flew, you never quite got used to that extraordinary beauty.

In Hamburg airport the exaltation collapsed. Hal mysteriously disappeared in some local confusion over luggage, and we waited, scattered about a crowded, overheated, airless, featureless space. Every movement meant a barked ankle on a luggage-trolley. No-one knew what was happening. Disgruntlement quickly spread. No-one spoke, unless to ask what the ––– was going on. Vitality ebbed away.

Hal reappeared, with two young men of strange appearance, and called us round him in the tight space. Enervation almost overcame manners: we could hardly be bothered to attend politely to what was obviously going to be a speech of welcome, probably of Germanic length. Why couldn't we get to the hotel? But one of the young Germans gave a crisp, brisk, better-English-than-the-English speech of welcome, and stopped. A colossal explosion of noise, of drums and whistles and horns and cries some fifty yards away brought swirling fantastic figures through the luggage-trapped airport crowd, to meet us, and lead us out in welcome. There were clown-figures and grotesques amazingly on stilts, whose faces were intent on making *us* feel wanted and happy and important to Ham-

The RSC welcomed at Hamburg airport by the Odin Teatret from Denmark.

burg. Feelings, having floundered on the bottom in mud spurted up in delight: this bizarre ceremony was beautifully timed.

Outside on the pavement by the coaches the energetic troupe gave us a performance, a mixture of leaping dance, acrobatics, clowning and stilt-work, to the incessant rhythms of drums, whistles and toots. We stood, trolleys and all. It was funny, and moving. The Odin Teatret from Helstebro in Denmark, like the RSC a part of the Festival about to open in Hamburg, the *Theater der Nationen*, was doing all this for our welcome and delight. Jill wept with happiness, and was not alone.

On the bus, another little speech of welcome, and two good items of news: the Festival organizers, knowing how difficult it is for actors to get meals after the show has come down, had arranged a marquee in the marketplace for midnight meals; and bookings for RSC were at 96%. (My own later attempt to get a meal in that marquee was a failure; and the figure of 96% turned out to be very misleading.)

Journal. Hotel Bellevue, An der Alster, Hamburg. 3.30, Wednesday. Suffering badly from what I'm learning to call transition-blues: but lonely and homesick as well, and hate this tour. Have been sold a pup, clearly. The tour is badly put together, badly organized. The hotels are far too expensive: I am, after all, financing myself. This room is sunless and noisy. How can I write a good book about such an uncelebratory experience? I suppose I could, even now, go home. I sit on the bed, head in hands, and groan. Distinctly hear my wife's voice asking 'When did you last eat?' Work out that it was a croissant and a cup of coffee at 7.30: with the change of clock, 6.30. I unpack, shower, and eat two oranges and a Marsbar. Things look a lot better.

The hotel Reception asks me to take a phone call: Maureen in Stratford – she is puzzled. She is ringing the Thalia-Theater, who say they have never heard of the RSC. I too am puzzled. Alistair, Basher, Di and the rest have gone on ahead, I know, and should be hard at work getting in. Odd.

I walked to the Thalia-Theater – and straight into a steaming row. At the stage-door was Desmond, and we neither of us got any change at all from the stage-door-keeper, who very obviously did not want to know us or let us through. A passing stage-technician said that he could take us to a girl and two men. In a distant office, sitting round a table, were Di, Alistair and Basher. They had arrived only a little ahead. They were pleased to see us but strangely muted. A young Englishman called Ralph, an Assistant Director at the Thalia-Theater, constantly dialled at a telephone. Nothing much was being said, but clearly something was wrong. Di explained. All the RSC stage-crew – except Philip who couldn't be found – had been sent off from Brussels on a very early coach to Schiphol to catch an early flight to Hamburg, to start the get-in in good time. In Holland, their driver had taken a wrong turn and taken them to Rotterdam instead of Amsterdam: they had caught their flight with not even a minute in hand and so had had no time in the duty-free shop.

They had booked quickly into the Hamburg hotel and gone to the Thalia-Theater. Walking round the building looking for the stage-door they had seen lavish advertising and photographs of *The Three Musketeers*, *The Idiot*, and Stoppard's *Schmutziger Wäsche*, among other things, but not a trace of the promotional pictures carefully sent by the RSC a month before. There was not a *Coriolanus* poster to be seen. The printed theatre programme on display outside, moreover, though it showed the RSC performances, gave also an additional matinée performance on Sunday. Worse, much worse, – indeed, catastrophic, – an extra performance of *The Three Musketeers* was announced for Thursday – tomorrow – when the RSC's contract had included, as it always did, a night without performance for the get-in and lighting.

Inside, allowed on to the stage, they discovered that it was three metres shorter than they had been told, which meant, among other things, that the iron would come down on top of the small walls. The lighting-board, they were told, had broken down.

Something had gone very wrong with the arrangements. Of all that was wrong, the single most serious matter was the additional *Three Musketeers* performance. (The *Intendant* [Director] of the theatre. Boy Gobert himself, later claimed that the contract, which this extra performance so blatantly breached, had been between the *Theater der Nationen* organizers and the RSC, and that the Thalia-Theater knew nothing of it.) Alistair telephoned Bill Wilkinson in Stratford, who then, by phone, put the matter bluntly to Gobert. There were only three possibilities: cancel the intrusive *Three Musketeers* last performance; cancel the first night of *Coriolanus*; or work all through Tuesday night to get the *Musketeers* out and *Coriolanus* in – though it was doubtful whether the German unions would allow all-night work. Meanwhile, the stage-size affair was sorted out; the Thalia had not taken out two rows of seats as they had promised, and had not built the extra fore-stage they were committed in writing to providing. (There was a tangle of possibilities why this had not been done. Either the Festival, or the Thalia, had not understood, or wanted to avoid the loss of revenue: and the suddenly-put-in *Musketeers* had also got in the way.) Everyone on the RSC side was very puzzled.

Jan de Blick had arranged an interpreter, Jenny Scollar, for the rest of the tour, all in German-speaking areas. Her work in the next forty-eight hours could not always have been pleasant, as feelings on both sides ran high.

In Brussels, meanwhile, Philip had woken up late in the morning in his room at the Palace Hotel to find everyone gone, escept Alan who was due to fly to Hamburg later. Philip, after the get-out, had gone to bed in the later small hours for a little sleep, expecting to be called. But the hotel reception mistook his room, and not a single message got through. So Philip emerged at mid-day a little more rested, and he and Alan spent a pleasant, low-key afternoon in Brussels, part of it looking on at an occasion in the Grande Place with a band playing, twenty-four motorcycles, a motorcade of Mercedes limousines, a battalion of soldiers lined up with rifles, and some very important people getting wet in a sudden violent shower as they got out of the cars and sprinted to a café.

Journal 6.30. p.m. At the theatre, I did manage to make some arrangements to see the management tomorrow morning. I walked back by the Alster in the chill evening sunlight: pretty boats on the lake, daffodils and ducks by the shore, willows just beginning to show leaf, the song of birds above the traffic noise. Hamburg – now I have food inside me – seems 'a goodly city', like Antium. Chatted to Philip Dunbar outside the hotel: he felt that Alan was worried about the Festival, feeling the Germans would not appreciate this *Coriolanus*.

On the following morning, Thursday, the difficulties in the theatre were just as intense. The lorries had arrived, but Alistair was refusing to unload them. The Thalia administration wanted the *Musketeers* set to be taken down, the RSC lorries to be unloaded, and for the crews to build the set on stage until two o'clock. Then, they said, it could be lit until four o'clock, when it could all be taken down again, and the *Musketeers* set replaced, and next morning it could all be put back and the lighting finished. The RSC crew insisted that that would not work. The German officials, Philip told me, insisted that it would work: 'Look,' they said, 'we are used to a very heavy repertory here, we are very good . . . you do not understand. Why are you not unloading and building? Then the lighting will be very quick. We know *Coriolan*, and we have all the lighting-cues already on tape from our own show. You do not understand.'

As a compromise, it was agreed that if the dock could be cleared, the unloading would proceed as far as that: it meant handling everything twice, taking it from dock to stage, but that could not be avoided. A great deal of persuasion of the Thalia management was necessary to get even as far as that. Moreover, agreement had been reached so that both the four RSC stage-staff and a second German crew could work over that night. Nobody wanted to cancel anybody's performance.

The official opening of the *Theater der Nationen* in the big Hamburg Schau-spielhaus at 11.00 am played to capacity and, for part of the event at least, to television cameras and lights. There were four speeches: from the Mayor of Hamburg, Herr Klose; from the Director of the Schauspielhaus, Ivan Nagel; from Walter Scheel, West German President; and from the most celebrated of modern German theatre directors, Peter Zadek (whose recent *Othello* with a nude Desdemona, and *The Winter's Tale* with live sheep, 'slime' and blood, were still much talked of). Marcel Marceau performed solo mimes of great brilliance. Walter Scheel, urbane, witty and accomplished, polished in his modesty, graced the occasion. Peter Zadek began by clutching his neck and murmuring how *could* one follow live theatre (Marceau had just performed) by intellectualization about the art? He developed a somewhat rambling thesis about the festive aspect of live theatre. Extremes of expression even in playing Shakespeare were evidence that German theatre was fighting its way out of its ghetto. He spoke for something under half an hour, his speech frequently punctuated by little bursts of girlish applause from various parts of the house. Marceau then gave a major piece, contrasting the present and the future, amusingly and movingly, to final music and stage-pictures not unlike the last reel of the film *2001*, at the end magically disappearing apparently into an infinity of distance at the back of the stage. After his curtain-calls, the house-lights came up and everyone rose. But the theatre suddenly erupted with noise from all parts, the drums and whistles and horns which the RSC recognized from Hamburg airport. Through all auditorium en-trances on all levels the Odin Teatret actors swung in towards the stage, some even walking the edges of the galleries and swooping down on ropes. People who had left the auditorium rushed back, and others crowded in. The Danes, still banging and blowing, formed up on stage, and then performed that same act that they had given us, while the huge audience stood and shouted and continuously applauded.

Hamburg that afternoon seemed to be full of displaced RSC actors wandering a little indecisively, unused to such liberty. The sun shone, even at times warmly. I went to the Festival headquarters, to see if I could get some of the photographs of the Danes performing on stage. The Festival centre in the old Markthalle, a tatty run-down building now full of big cardboard signs, had an atmosphere like the Fringe office at the Edinburgh Festival, though rather more heavy. No-one had a second to spare. In the Press Office were smiling young people and on every trestle-table, three telephones, all ringing.

At mid-day Alan, Maxine, Graham and Bill had been entertained to lunch by the young, dynamic Mayor in his suite overlooking the Alster, the well-named Schöne Aussicht. The reception was in honour of the RSC and the members of Peking Opera, who were visiting the West for the first time for 24 years, and for whom Hamburg was the first engagement. I heard later from Graham what a splendid occasion this lunch had been, only faintly marred for him by his nervousness at sitting next to a most heavily-serious German drama-critic. Half-way through, the occasion had been enlivened by the unexpected arrival of Peter Zadek. Before his present tremendous fame in Germany, Zadek had worked obscurely in various local theatres in England, where he had trained. Graham, apparently finding his face teasingly familiar, over coffee suddenly located their previous encounter. 'I know you now,' he cried, putting a big hand on his shoulder, – 'Pontypridd Rep.!'

The opening celebrations of the Festival included a grand reception in the Plaza Hotel, one of the most luxurious in Europe. This affair was also the official civic reception in honour of the Chinese; all Festival members were invited. The party could not start until the Chinese show, playing at the Schauspielhaus, had come down. Just before midnight Maxine, Di and I made our own unregarded entrance up a wide circular staircase, to join elegant Hamburg ladies in long dresses holding glasses of blue champagne-cocktail, standing on a wide landing. Before us was a vast carpeted ball-room, with thatched booths down the centre attended by chefs serving hot food, and further tables with cold meats, cheeses, fruits, breads, and drinks everywhere. But before we could move in, applause began below, and up the circular stairs fluttered the Chinese dancers in twos, the girls in pretty dresses, the men in grey suits, all diminuitive, broadly smiling, applauding us applauding them with an infectious delight, moving into the ballroom between the hosts lining the way, like a flight of delicate birds.

We went in, and in the crowd found Graham, deeply not listening to a solemn German. He saw us, and strode across, clasping me to him. 'Rescue me!' he hissed. 'I had that man all through lunch, and he has absolutely no sense of humour!' Carrying loaded plates and refilled glasses, we moved through the most cosmopolitan and dressed-to-extremes crowd I have ever been in. Older Hamburgians in full evening dress stood near touring actors in best posh, i.e. a clean shirt, or young fringe-theatre students in wild extravaganzas of costume, or lack of it. Arthur and Richard, who with others had been to the sold-out Peking show by the simple method of walking in and sitting down in empty seats (of which there were plenty) were jovially trying to convey their huge enthusiasm for what they had seen to five Chinese men standing smiling in a row. Arthur, with urgent cries, pulled across a girl who interpreted. Arthur wanted to know all about the fights, continually telling us poor creatures who had failed in life by not being there just how fantastic they were, and how, as in our own show, all the fighting depended on trust. We asked how long they had trained, which seemed to be about seven years. They all expressed delight at being guests, and talking with the RSC people – it seemed impossible to out-do them in happy, humble courtesy. There was much swapping of badges, RSC for Peking Opera. There was more sense of internationality, of social, cross-cultural freedom, and of true decorum, than I had ever met at a party before; and at the centre of it all were the tiny

Boy Gobert as Coriolan in the Thalia-Theater version of *Coriolanus* written and directed by Hans Hollman.

Chinese, smiling, smiling. They were photographed, by a Chinese man with a flash-camera, standing with Arthur, and then with Charlie and Graham, towering above.

Journal. Friday 27 April 8.30 am. One night recently – can't remember which – I had an early night and got to bed at one-thirty. Last night it was three. Odd to be not only surviving but flourishing on four hours sleep a night. Yesterday I succeeded in changing rooms, and am now in a sunny, quiet and friendly spot, reading the Brecht version of *Coriolanus*, and Günter Grass' treatment of the first scene. Downstairs after breakfast found a big box full of Festival and Hamburg documents which we all should have had two days ago. It would have made life a little easier for everyone to have had them yesterday.

At the theatre I met Margaret Mieruch, and sat in her office and looked at photographs of their production of *Coriolan*, and a copy of the text. Margaret, assistant to the Deputy Director, Dr Gerhard Blasche, was never-failingly helpful to me though as I discovered later she was passionately loyal to the Thalia-Theater, and unhappy about the RSC.

The Intendant of the Thalia-Theater, Boy Gobert, himself one of Germany's top-ranking actor-directors, had taken the lead in their version of the play prepared and directed by Hans Hollmann, opening in October 1977. (An earlier Hollmann version had been played in 1971 at the Residenztheater in Munich.) I had seen the booklet about the production briefly in Brussels: but not until I shuffled through a box of pictures and glanced through the text, did I realize that the title '*Coriolan von Hans Hollmann frei nach Shakespeare*' was the truth – it was Hollmann's play. Shakespeare had been severely cut, and many new characters, and many new short scenes, had been added. It seemed to work on a principle of historical snap-shots with words. The modern battle-scenes, with second world-war atrocities demonstrated, and a medical examination of the troops for VD, for example, seemed especially unhappy under that title. Some character-names, and some parts of some speeches were the same, but the drastic shortening and re-writing, and the great shift in emphasis, removed it far from Shakespeare. It was a modern, and in my opinion offensive, pageant by Hollmann.

Margaret arranged for me to talk with Gerhard Blasche. I sat in his office for a long part of the morning with him, drinking coffee from pretty china, with mineral-water accompanying in the Viennese way. Gobert joined us for a while. They were kind and forthcoming. Both had close associations with the Burgtheater, so discussion of Terry's work was informed. They gave me some insight into the more recent history of the Thalia, how from the mid-seventies they had moved away from the then characteristically political German theatre to put on unfamiliar plays. They had developed a strong and loyal following, but were caught between town politics and hostile and influential critics, on *Der Spiegel* and *Die Zeit* in particular.

I asked about their *Coriolan*. They explained that Hollmann took out everything which made the audience sympathize with Coriolanus, and tried instead to show the danger of '*Spezialismus*', of being a specialist in war in particular, and how this allows the rise of the power of the Tribunes. In the war-sequences the costumes went through the ages, and in each scene between the Tribunes and the tailor (invented by Hollmann of course) their dress became more and more like that of modern trades-union officials. They had taken the play to an annual workers' drama festival at Recklinghausen in the Ruhr. This festival started just after the war, under an agreement whereby in exchange for coal, Hamburg gave them experience of art. It was taking me some time to begin to fathom the political power of cultural economics in North Germany. I was to have other vivid illustrations: but for the moment I was overwhelmed by the impossibility of Jack Jones or Arthur Scargill agreeing to send Newcastle coal to London in exchange for a couple of plays from the Aldwych. At Recklinghausen, older people had reported that the Hollmann play had given them a chance to think over the past, recognizing possible reactions to a Fascist experience. The trades-union officials there had told Gobert, 'You shit all over us, and we love it'. The play had also gone to Warsaw, where many people had left during the first performance. Gobert explained that this was because they were so used to uniforms there that they thought that they themselves were being caricatured. The German ambassador to Poland, however, said it had helped him in his work. There was a lot of anti-German intellectualism at the time, and it showed that the Germans were not all Nazis.

All this did seem to me to be rather a long way from Shakespeare. It was bizarre to sit so comfortably, elegantly exchanging sophisticated talk, while at my elbow a large television screen showed the set in place on stage, my good friends Di, Alistair, Neil, Philip, Basher, Garry and Johnny O'Mahoney moving about on it, and lighting proceeding. I could not imagine what physical and emotional brute force had got things to that state of readiness: *Musketeers* had come down a lot less than twelve hours before.

Gobert and Blasche explained that they were presently leaving the Thalia, moving to the Schiller-Theater in Berlin. I saw a copy of the evening paper *Hamburger Abendblatt* for 2 November 1978 in which the news was announced. The first three pages were devoted to the matter, with accounts of Gobert's plays, comments from everywhere, including the canteen, and many pictures of him. This was in fact Gobert's escape from the politics of Hamburg. Ivan Nagel, who had successfully re-established the Schauspielhaus, had recently been dismissed as Director, effectively by the Senate, in a political war heavily involving the Press: the Festival was in fact his last triumph. Who was to be his successor? The field was assumed to have a front-runner, Gobert, whom the cheaper, more right-wing Springer press supported as being more conservative, more pleasing-the-public: he would, it was thought, combine the two different theatres, Thalia and Schauspielhaus. But he accepted the invitation to the Schiller-Theater in Berlin, and, it was said, made a laughing-stock of the Senate. Gobert and Blasche are both great admirers of Peter Zadek, and will get him to direct their first play in Berlin: Zadek is something of a hero, too, of the leftist press.

I asked what had happened to the RSC's publicity-pictures which should have been outside the theatre. Blasche simply said that their disappearance was the fault of the Festival. (Bill and others had been told that the pictures had been locked in a Thalia cupboard; unfortunately the key was missing.) He took me front of house, explaining that the theatre seats 1014, a little smaller than both the Burg in Vienna and the Schiller in Berlin. The only bit of the building to survive the war was some woodwork in the foyer. The theatre dates from 1843, the present building being opened in 1912, and rebuilt in 1946.

Journal. Hamburg. Friday. By arrangement, I met Graham at one, and we walked through pedestrian precincts and over uncrowded city roads looking for lunch, he clutching his Arden *Coriolanus*, my notebook open and ready, both of us heavily over-coated, stopping in the chill dull weather to stare at the coming summer season's 'in' garments in shop-windows, drapes of shocking pink and scarlet hanging on otherwise naked forms.

We settled in a *Gaststätte* where habitual lunch-time card-players were not quite sure about us, one or two of Graham's more powerfully-felt demonstrations of a point causing sour looks behind him. He spoke, as so many actors did, to me, on that tour, with special recollection of sayings of Tyrone Guthrie – that the meanest spear-holder, or one-liner, was more important than any of the direction; that as soon as the play started, the actors were like racehorses brought to the starting-point, and they had to be in superb condition. He talked too about the sheer size, now, of RSC management. Again, as most did, he spoke with affection for Terry's company, which had been together since the *Henry 6's* were young. The company spirit was so high in the *Henry 6's* because there were so many good people in it, in both senses. Someone, he said had come into the green-room at Stratford during the *Henry 6's* and asked Graham if there were factions in the company. I said, 'Of *course* there are factions – but anyone can join'. He believed that some of the spirit of adventure and happiness in that company was not now present: they felt cheated by experiences in Brussels and Amsterdam. When he had dined, had sufficient Käsebrot, and was still drinking coffee, I asked about Menenius.

Graham had started work on the part without former impressions, having never seen the play. Terry had suggested that Menenius was Son of Falstaff, rejection and all. Graham's experience was that though, of course, at the end of scene 18, when he is in extremity, he goes to heal himself with food, (Volumnia by contrast will starve – 'anger's my meat') Menenius was unlike Falstaff; he hadn't put on armour, even.

This play did not show the strong lines of the Falstaff-Hal relationship, but Graham pointed to virtually the last time Coriolanus ever speaks with him, when he is leaving after the banishment, at the very end of scene 17. They share a joke about 'foot' and 'hand', exposing a mutual body; that, he felt, was the nearest they got to a Falstaff-Hal position.

Menenius, he felt, was a popular patrician with the common touch, like Harold

Confrontation in the Senate. Left to right: Second Roman Senator (Mike Hall), Cominius (Bernard Brown), Menenius (Graham Crowden), Coriolanus (Alan Howard), First Roman Senator (Paul Imbusch), Sicinius Velutus (John Burgess), Junius Brutus (Oliver Ford-Davies).

Macmillan. He liked the Citizens. He didn't relate to the Tribunes because he didn't choose to do so. His hostile attitude to them in scene 11 is a lynch-pin of that part of the play; from the moment Coriolanus returns after the wars, and the Tribunes begin to get their power, Menenius, having attacked them, is left more and more outside the action, without voice, until in scene 15 Volumnia takes over. He is kept back, Graham felt, so that he can make his later appeal in the Rejection scene with the highest fresh charge. He is approached to make what amounts to a sacrifice, asked to *test* himself and his love, in those scenes 24 and 25. He dreads that test of the relationship with the young man. He takes his chance, and loses. 'So I chose to play scene 27, which is a little bit cut, as if he had *mal de tête*: he speaks non-sequiturs, he speaks terrible things, he doesn't care, it is a hollow rejoicing: "Hark, how *they* joy"! he says. He is a comic-tragic figure.'

Graham saw it a⌣ a deeply religious play about believing in truth, about someone with a naïve concept of truth. 'Shakespeare gives in Coriolanus the naked steel blue flame of truth – Aufidius is a second-rater.' This came out in the Shakespearean see-saw, where Volumnia's 'Do your will' at the end of scene 15 itself set up the next (banishment) scene. He felt John Burgess was very, very good in that scene, low-keying it, putting the violence of the crowd on to Coriolanus, getting the power of an 'and *shall*'. Alan, Graham reported, had said he felt that Coriolanus had no means of contact at all with the Tribunes.

We developed an idea that I was formulating, that Menenius is a pillar of Rome, and attracts such imagery to himself, having something of *Henry 6 Part Two* Gloucester's strength. In that play it takes all the peers a long time to kill the Protector – a play and a half – even though, like Menenius, he doesn't fight. Graham had disagreed with Abdel Farrah's suggestion that Gloucester should carry a sword, saying that the Protector of England wouldn't – and in any case he,

Graham, hated clobber and always tripped over swords. (He said, incidentally, that designers can always tell you a great deal about a play – adding, stagily *sotto voce* 'often far more than a director', rolling his eyes to see if some of his former directors were listening: the Hamburg locals, without stopping their cards, stared.) He based Menenius partly on the choleric side of Gloucester. He was very interested in the fact that in both *Part One* and *Part Two* of *Henry 6* Gloucester is in charge of the boy-king, but wasn't quite the *statesman*: rather than succeed in coping with his turbulent peers, he stuck to his own kind of truth. He was loved by the common people, betrayed by the great ones' treachery through his love for his wife. Menenius similarly is not politically as effective as Volumnia; faced with approaching disaster, he feels it is his duty to put his love at risk. Gloucester's strength was his refusal to move away from basic decencies, and he went down, like Menenius.

Coriolanus was the last of Shakespeare's tragedies. *Part Two* of *Henry 6* was right at the start of his writing life. Falstaff, coming in the middle, points both ways, forming, Graham felt, a direct link.

As we walked the streets again, Graham explained how ill he had been in Vienna, and in the break, and how alarmed he had felt in Amsterdam about his own health. Only for that reason was he glad to be going back to London first thing on Sunday.

Alone, I tramped off to the Markthalle again. I asked if I could have pictures of the Peking Opera performers at the party last night – I particularly wanted the shots of our actors with theirs. I, somewhat absent-mindedly, said that I could always write to the Chinese photographer after the tour. There was silently held up to me an envelope from Peking: the home address, in the beautiful Chinese calligraphy in green ink, looked like a summer garden in full leaf.

I got back to the theatre to find it dark, and no-one about, and an atmosphere of intense disturbance hanging about on stage, where there should have been a rehearsal. That, I felt, was a situation in which I did *not* want to have a furious Alan discover me lurking, so I fled and steadied myself in my hotel room with scholarly book-work in the afternoon sunshine.

I heard later from Philip and others what had happened. Both crews, English and German, had worked overnight to get *Musketeers* out and *Coriolanus* in, with mutual admiration. Everyone on the RSC side agreed that the Thalia crew was extremely good; helpful and willing and understanding what was wanted, though they did keep saying that the RSC was crazy to travel with such a huge set, which they would never do. They had not believed it was so huge. In the morning by the time the night-shift went off at seven, the Germans were exhausted. A new shift came on and were equally good, and everything in every technical department was going swimmingly: the second crew was excellent, and Basher had never been so far ahead with the lighting. It helped that they had very good

The Stage Manager (Philip Hoare) in characteristic pose.

equipment, and a memory-board (broken, certainly, but easily mended), almost identical to the one at Stratford. One of their electricians, Tom, was a Canadian and a godsend, everyone agreed, in that he understood all the equipment and both languages perfectly. The set and lighting were on the way to looking better than they had ever done on the tour.

A rehearsal had been called for two-thirty. Precisely at that time the super-efficient German crew suddenly began to complain that – as lighting was proceeding – they could not see to rehearse the movements of the walls. The RSC staff explained that the trucks were not heavy, there was adequate light, and there were marks on the floor anyway. The Germans insisted on consulting higher authority, but no word came. In the absence of such higher authority, they did nothing. Alan, who had come back from a television interview for the rehearsal, was not pleased. Feeling began to run very high. Such problems had been unknown even with casual student labour in Brussels. At four o'clock, when nothing whatsoever had been accomplished, it was announced that there was a union regulation that all the crews had to have a two-hour tea-break, starting at once. Alan's anger was towering.

The RSC, astonished and bewildered by the Thalia-Theater behaviour, cancelled all rehearsals except for the usual brief run-through with Alan on the walls and the Alan/Charlie fight, which would be at six, even though many of the cast needed to be getting ready then. In any case, the rehearsal was for the German follow-spot operators – though they had plots, one actor in black leather looks very like another. At six, these two routines went smoothly, and were finished before six-fifteen. It was later understood by RSC stage-crew, working alongside their German friends, that such a two-hour break had never been heard of before, and was not in union regulations.

The atmosphere when the show went up at seven-thirty was highly charged, not helped by the fact that there were many empty seats. I stood for a moment at the front of the equivalent of the dress-circle just before the house-lights went out, and noted that attendance in many parts of the house could only be described as thin. Not that it helped much, I noted too that it was by far the best-dressed audience we had had on the tour. Hamburg is a very prosperous city, and the younger people there have known nothing but security and wealth, taking these as a right reward for their part in the *Wirtschaftswunder*. In the city I felt, consequently, an easy confidence which did not debase into arrogance. Hamburg seemed to me to be full of beautifully dressed, tall, good-looking younger people: and many of the best-dressed and best-looking were in that first-night audience.

Technically, the show was magnificent. It had never been better-lit, and looked stunning. Cues of all kinds seemed to have an exceptional *finesse*. The tensions of the day burst through in wonderful playing. The audience was unusually lively and alert. For example, in the middle of scene 14, when Menenius dismisses Coriolanus' mounting point about the folly of the Greeks in giving corn to the people gratis, he punctures a political tirade in embryo with a 'Well, well, no more of that' – and at that on this night he got a round of applause. Hamburg, it seemed, had had too much of heavy political points in their drama.

That was the last thin house we had in Hamburg. Remembering later the enraptured audience at the end, I understood why. I had not known such excited spectators – or such long applause, though that is part of the German tradition – nor overheard such enthusiastic comments.

In the upstairs foyer the reception given by the Thalia-Theater in honour of the RSC had one area of relaxed enjoyment, that around the British Ambassador to the Federal Republic, Sir Oliver Wright, who had come from Bonn especially to be with us. It was difficult to spot His Excellency. I looked hard at one moment at a row of contented RSC stage-staff sitting on a wide stair, and realized that Sir Oliver was sitting happily eating and chatting between John Moore and Jake. Elsewhere the atmosphere was a bit prickly. Everyone, led by Alan, wondered why the bad situations of the afternoon had developed without a word from – or sign of – the Intendant. I crossed the floor to ask Gobert how he had enjoyed the performance: after a diplomatic pause he said that he felt there was a lot to be said for performing Shakespeare with heavy cuts. He had just publicly, and lavishly, embraced Alan. Gobert and I were photographed. Gobert quickly told the photographer that I was *not* Alan Howard, and all interest in me evaporated on the spot. Attempts to photograph a scowling Alan with Gobert and the Ambassador failed. Trevor Nunn had flown in, and Bill had also now arrived. Gobert made a speech of welcome. He said that Shakespeare had been a German national poet for two

Maxine Audley.

hundred and fifty years, and, being in German before Goethe and Schiller wrote, and influencing them deeply, he was felt to be especially German. But they had to remember that the cradle of Shakespeare was not Germany, and guest performances in English helped this.

The evening was not very much enjoyed by some, though the RSC technical staff got on well with some Thalia staff.

From the Journal of Paul Basson (Young Martius), aged 10. Friday 27 April. A Boring Day. On Friday we woke up and had breakfast then we did some school. After school we went to the British Consul to have our passports stamped. Then we saw the theatre and took some photographs of it. When we had taken some pictures we had lunch and went back to the hotel and did the rest of the school work. Then we had tea at a King Burger and then dropped Stephen off at the theatre and went back to the hotel and got into bed.

On Saturday, notices began to appear. The *Hamburger Abendblatt* critic said that the RSC plays Shakespeare from the text, and was greeted in Hamburg with tumultuous jubilation (*'vom Publikum stürmisch umjubelt'*). He contrasted this with Zadek's 'disrespectful association with the poet from Stratford', and with the Gobert/Hollmann production. 'Our English visitors played Shakespeare pure, rolling every word, every sigh, on their tongues, and showed the continentals once more what the art of theatre means in England.'

One afternoon, Maxine told me that at the beginning she had remembered seeing Olivier's Coriolanus in 1959, but couldn't remember his Volumnia. She had fished out her old programme and found it had been Edith Evans, and began to be alarmed. If *she* had made so little impact on her in the part, what hope, Maxine wondered, for herself? One key to Volumnia, she felt, was her possessiveness; this child was *hers*: Maxine was convinced that she had handled his birth alone, simply gone out into the woods by herself. There is never any mention of a husband. She thought of mothers: her own; the mother in *The Manchurian Candidate*; Gloria Connors (who, hearing her son had secretly got married, had said 'I always told him he could'); there was a Jewish-American mother in this woman, she felt, like the one in *Portnoy's Complaint*. She had found it exciting that costume-designs and even set-details were waiting until Terry and Abdel saw what the actors were doing with the characters so that, for example, after a first idea that in scene 3 Virgilia would be standing sewing at a large tapestry, that gradually shrank until it became the foot or two of light white cloth Jill sat and sewed on her knee every night, compelling concentration on the beauty and peace of both women in the simple domestic scene.

Working on the size of the emotion had been exceptionally interesting. Terry had told her to 'see' her son in Olympian power in her 'vision' in scene 3 as if there were a television screen at the back of the auditorium: that moment was still domestic. She had been helped by filming for Melvyn Bragg's television *South Bank Show* part of scene 26 (the pleading scene) in which she had found very moving the discovery of almost a miniature expression, coming down from something in her that was harsh, even granity almost. Going back to scene 15 after that, she had been able to work on a feeling of much more intimacy between herself and Alan, and Graham. She too found Terry's gift for picking people who work well together extraordinary and valuable. All sorts of people had given each other notes: Bille Brown's to her had been of particular value all through.

We talked about the parallel between Volumnia and Lady Macbeth. Maxine pointed out that both started in high relationship with their men. Lady M's man gets cold feet, and becomes hard work, but then takes over as they change places. Volumnia's child also rebels, but in the end goes very much his own way, from 'I will not do't' in scene 15 to which he gets the typical maternal reaction to a headstrong child. (Volumnia from that point, I felt, moves back into silence, until, like Lady M, she makes a powerful final appearance which is contrary to the previous movement.)

Maxine was interested in something Alan had started to do in Vienna, and developed since. In his last lines of farewell in scene 17 he took to coming more eagerly back from the gates as if a new idea had struck him suddenly – that he can take Virgilia, Volumnia, Menenius and Cominius, his four emotional stars, with him; the words said on a rising tone of excited query, with a pause after 'touch':

> Come, my sweet wife, my dearest mother, and
> My friends of noble touch . . .

But no-one responded, so Alan resumed the strong formal, faintly sardonic, farewell note for the next words, 'when I am forth . . .'. It had been a point of great importance to them all in rehearsal to try to understand why they did not go with him anyway, or at least why they made no effort to persuade him to stay. Virgilia in the following scene adds to Volumnia's command to Sicinius 'You shall stay too' with 'I would I had the power / To say so to my husband'. As Maxine put it, if only Volumnia could have said at that point of farewell, 'Boo-hoo, I love you – take us with you': but her pride is in the way; and in that area of the play, she, like Menenius, is deprived of speech.

And at the end, unlike Lady M, she cannot go mad: as Maxine said, she is too old-fashioned for that. She cannot fling around in despair, but is simply bitter and puzzled, shattered but not destroyed, asking where she went wrong, but not fundamentally changed. This understanding was one of the sources of Terry's imaginative stroke of Volumnia's presentation of Young Martius as his father again in miniature, at the climax of the procession at the end of the penultimate scene.

She, like everyone else who spoke to me, was fascinated by the play's extraordinary tricks of language, as it seizes on verbal cues like 'What then?', and 'shall', playing with conversational repetitions with a modern author's touch: and at the other extreme concocting extraordinary verbs like 'mountebank', 'virgin'd', 'fidiussed,' and flinging up amazing elaborations of associated words. Some of these almost Baroque decorations, I suggested, sat more strangely than usual in relation to the great gaps in the play where detail about large matters was simply missing and questions were simply left unanswered. And like every actor in the company she was constantly struck by the way people found the right phrase in their mouths, all the time – the mark of a very great play.

Her final comment was on the concentration that the play, and her part, demanded. As Terry had first reminded them, and as none of them could ever avoid, nobody in this play ever talks about anything but one man. Maxine said 'There's no Porter, no Gravedigger, no Fool: the play just goes relentlessly down the centre, all the time.' So she found something that had never happened to her before: whereas, when playing Lady M, for example, it was a help to relax and chat before going on, here she found she had to listen to the play constantly, all the time over the tannoy, had to keep an exact line on where they'd got to on stage, where they were going. If she didn't, in this play, she was lost.

For the second performance the house was full, lively and eager to respond from the beginning. They were rather more than lively in Maxine's last speech in scene 15. For a reason never explained, shouting broke out from two men near the front of the stalls, and after loud exchanges, and some urgent barracking from the audience, a small party left the theatre. Alan, on the first words of his next speech. 'Pray be content', was able to hold a pause and restore the audience's concentration. His last word in the scene, 'Mildly!', strikingly spat out as always, got an unusually enthusiastic round. By contrast, his grand upstage exit in the next scene, on 'There is a world elsewhere!' was very properly greeted with intense attention, the relaxation only coming with light, uneasy laughter on Barrie's 'The people's enemy is gone.' The act ended to as great applause as the company had heard, and the final applause of the evening lost very little on the previous night. After the show that night I went up to Graham's dressing-room to say goodbye: he was leaving next morning, and opening soon at the New Roundhouse with the Royal Exchange Company in Ibsen's *The Lady from the Sea*, with Vanessa Redgrave.

Watching, listening and talking with many people, I began to feel my way for the first time into the labyrinth of modern German reactions to Shakespeare in the theatre. I knew that there was a conflict of styles: among the followers of the Wieland Wagner approach the RSC production was instantly popular: but some modern German directors went for ever wilder and more extravagant irrelevances until the play disappeared in optical tricks, machinery, grotesque manipulation (why not a *Tempest* with four Prosperos on stage together?) and – above all – underplayed verbal rhetoric, substituting injected screams for continual full-voiced words for example, as Zadek had mentioned in his opening speech. I found that an anti-Zadek faction used the RSC production as a weapon. Some time before, I had fought my way, with difficulty and disbelief, through the review in the *Frankfurter Allgemeine* dated 21 February 1979 of Hansgünther Heyme's production of *Hamlet* in Cologne – now known all over Germany as 'the one with the videos', because there are eighteen black and white television screens on stage, (with thirty more as mock-ups), showing Hamlet's distorted face, or a programme transmitted at the time. At one point, Dietrich Fischer-Dieskau is heard in a Schumann *lied*. In Hamburg, I heard a little more about this production. Hamlet's words are spoken over the sound-system by Heyme from a director's desk in the sixth or seventh row in the auditorium during most of the play. The actor playing Hamlet begins the play speaking, but after the scene with the ghost he is mute and only moves about the stage adjusting the television cameras or, more commonly, chalking his silhouette on a grey canvas. Heyme then himself joins him on stage and they perform symbolic parallel movements. At the end, both are wheeled naked on to the stage lying on hospital trolleys, their

intestines spilling out. Throughout the play, the scenery includes a horse sus-
pended by its legs from the roof and bleeding into a wine-glass. The designer was
Wolf Vostell, a big 'happening artist' of the sixties, now, I'm told, 'into' all sorts of
technical things like video and films and theatre. I'm told too that either this
Hamlet 'blows your mind', or you hate it.

One word is everywhere, following round the most famous German directors –
Zadek, Stein in Berlin, Wendt in Munich, Peymann in Stuttgart (now going to
Bochum, where Zadek was) Noelte and Heyme. It sums up both the desperate
search for a new approach and that combination of politics and economics which
seems to control so much of German theatre life – as it was put to me, 'Who had
heard of Bochum before Zadek went there?' A production that all Germany is
talking about puts that town on the map. In a divided country, where at least four
cities are rivals for the title of capital (Bonn, Berlin, Hamburg and Munich) the
sense that everything is happening in one spot gives that spot a great lead. So the
word that follows direction about is *Skandal.* Heyme, now in Cologne, previously
in Stuttgart, was famous for his productions having more stink-bombs thrown at
them than anyone else's. At the more ordinary local level, happily, the German
production of Shakespeare has more concern with what Shakespeare wrote.

German theatres are more heavily subsidized than an Englishman can easily
imagine. I was told that the annual subsidy of one theatre was greater than the
entire Arts Council budget for all arts in the UK for one year. (However, German
friends always hasten to add that the figures do not compare, as, to be fair, the
Arts Council total should also include *all* cultural benefits, including such things
as the county library services.) Knowing the resulting pay and job-security of
actors and stage-crews, English theatre-people turn gently green. Yet in theatre
terms, the result is *Skandal*, for such vast outlays are political bludgeons, and the
enterprise of seeking prestige for its own sake necessarily breeds an invisible, and
therefore corruptible, power-struggle. It is not difficult to sense inside the artistic
endeavour a desperate need to justify. Peter Zadek said in his Festival speech that
theatre sometimes means driving the public to their limits, so that among other
things they can see where their limits are. All this seems a long way from the
Aldwych and Terry Hands and Peter Brook, whose current *Antony and Cleopatra*
lovingly draws out the text, and sheds precisely those trimmings which have been
mistaken for the play itself for so long.

Again, in German theatre, the press stands in a position quite different from
that in Britain. A performance is treated at solemn length, of course; but it is also
commented on in a tortuous, complex, introverted manner which is determinedly
'in' and at the same time carefully objective. The critic does not say 'I thought this
was good, that was terrible' but simply (no, not simply: no German drama critic
ever put anything simply!) makes objective, near-absolute, pronouncements.
And, of course, as we saw with the news of Gobert going to Berlin, he can reckon
on a lot of space. German friends express disappointment with British critics,

pointing out that a great German critic will do massive homework, studying the text and all available commentary for weeks. He has of course the space for such learning. He has too a quite different function in a disunited country with such an extreme theatrical range, conflicting theatre styles, partisan audiences, and a powerfully aligned press. Audiences in this climate have to have thick programme notes, and the critic's duty is to challenge the most basic concepts of theatre. Such a challenge can also be a matter of intense local, civic pride – as we were to find in Munich. For in Germany theatre for two hundred years has been a public forum for discussion of social and political problems; a social tool, in fact. Thus is High Seriousness wedded to Theatre. It must be more than entertainment. It must have a Message.

A visiting theatre-company gives everyone breathing-space. Even so, the German papers had difficulty with a production by a director, Terry Hands, many of whom were convinced was far out to the Left. I have heard, several times, Terry say with weary patience, 'We are not communist'. It would have been simpler for the German press if we had been so extreme: and in Paris, of course, Terry Hands is on the Right!

From Paul Basson's journal. Sunday 29 April. An Exciting Day. On Sunday we woke up and had breakfast. After breakfast we read and did some school work.

Then we went to the theatre to fetch Cynthia for lunch. When we had finished our lunch we went on the U-bahn to a Park. The park was really good it had an adventure playground in it and some water-games. One was that you had a ball tied to some string and you had a hose that sprayed water and you had to get the ball out of a hole and back in again. The other one was that you had a polystyrene brick and a hose and you had to try and score goals but it ended up in a water-fight, I got soaked.

Then we took the U-bahn back to the hotel.

Monday 30 April. *Die Welt* carried a major review. This started by dragging in the out-dated Jan Kott only to say that Terry Hands proves him wrong – this hero may arouse sympathy. It goes on to say that Alan Howard looks and acts like a rocker. In between it presents the outrageous notion that Terry Hands 'obviously found in recent English history, especially his country's present economic plight, reasons for his interpretation', for this Coriolanus 'despised the plebs because all they were interested in in wartime was booty and because even in peace they thought only of their own advantage – not of the well-being of the state'. Yet in spite of a climate of such smug, partisan insult, the review is profoundly appreciative, calling it 'a sensational production in German theatre terms'. The critic praises the depth of Howard's reading, 'cursing and railing' but refusing the spoils of war, in his element when fighting and 'so fair that he throws down his own sword after he has knocked his enemy's out of his hand'. The pleading scene shows that 'lust for war is not his inspiration'. 'Even more surprising than the unfashionable interpretation is the staging, which, judged by "progressive" standards, might be called conventional. There are no vistas, no elaborate stage machinery, opulent optical effects of revolutionary inspirations . . . In the mass scenes . . . there are never more than eight actors on stage at any one time. Only lighting effects are used to indicate that a change of scene has taken place. Everything else is left to language . . . The mimetic and gesticulatory expression of this simple yet fascinating performance is derived from language alone. . . . The Hamburg audience, spellbound till almost midnight, applauded thunderously – and rightly. This precision and accuracy, this fidelity to a classical original is something they never see in our theatre.'

The Hamburg edition of the popular *Bild-Zeitung*, with a lead-picture of Max-ine and Alan gave greatest prominence to *Coriolanus* in the Festival – and to the contrast with Hollmann's *Coriolan*, praising the RSC for not making the slightest attempt to alter Shakespeare 'for today'. 'They play him from the page – and it is sublime'. The *Hamburger Morgenpost*, offering 'hot tips for the theatre-struck' put the RSC first, 'an unforgettable experience of traditional English theatre'. The *Frankfurter Allgemeine* developed its critic's earlier analysis at Stratford 'an example of a new conservative style', with 'an aristocratic outsider triumphant in bloody beauty who makes a timid petty-bourgeois republic look ridiculous'. In Hamburg, Howard's 'male strip-tease', Coriolanus' relentless self-projection, was felt to be irritating. This important paper's tone was cool, saying that the production was hardly less unhistorical than Hollman's, and finally objecting to the Festival choosing to tangle matters by bringing as an example of ensemble-playing something approaching 'one-man theatre'.

Monday 10.30. I walk to the theatre in sudden thick darkness and a winter storm, and sit in Margaret Mieruch's office picking melting hailstones out of my hair. I am to discuss with Boy Gobert his considered view of our *Coriolanus*. He gives me the rest of the morning. I sit in comfort in his spacious, elegant office, vases of tulips lighting up the black-and-chrome of the décor. Twice he goes across the room to the phone: once to ask Blasche the meaning of *eitel* (we are discussing Alan) . . . 'conceited', he says with sorrow and satisfaction, 'conceited'. The next time he listens, and murmurs *'Bin nicht da'* ('I'm not in'). His summing-up was that the RSC had sent a B-team with an international star. At the end of our conversation, as I leave, I find Hal and Bill saying 'Goodbye' to Blasche on the landing, surprised to find that Gobert was in after all. Bill is going ahead to Berlin. Blasche hands over the missing publicity-photographs on their thick, big cards: the key to the cupboard had just been found.

That afternoon I went for the last time to the Markthalle, and got the telephone number of Mr Hu Yung-Chen, who would supply me with photographs of the Peking actors at the party, I was told. I went back to the Thalia and telephoned from Hal's office. 'Herr Hu?', I said, feeling rising hilarity when I had to repeat it. *'Ich bin mit dem Royal Shakspeare Company aus England . . .'* I put my question, but

The Tour Manager (Hal Rogers).

didn't make sense of the reply. Jenny Scollar's daughter Claire was in the office. She has perfect English and German, and she took over. I heard both sides of the conversation. There was no mistaking what Mr Hu was saying: there were no photographs. No photographs were taken at the party in the Plaza. No, our RSC actors were not photographed with the Peking Opera actors. It was useless for me to say that they were. That was the end of that.

The Festival, and *Coriolanus* in particular, attracted a great deal of attention in Germany. I have in front of me, as I write, press notices from a dozen news-papers, some syndicated and unoriginal, from Cologne, Wiesbaden, Heidelberg, Osnabrück, Saarbrücken and elsewhere. From Bielefeld there is a full notice. Most of them comment on the primacy of the spoken text, and the centrality of the hero, rather than class-war. Almost all find 'rockers' somewhere, and 'Superstar' qualities in Coriolanus himself.

It is clear to me that the world of Shakespeare is not so alive in modern Germany as modern Germans would have us believe. Recalling Bernard Levin's judgement that this was 'the strongest, clearest and most consistent Shakespeare I have seen anywhere for years', I realize that what is central and 'Shakespearean' about the production is being quite missed: a whole area is blank – there is no discussion of a *tragic* hero, nor of the pressures of high, formal Jacobean tragedy. Talk of Superstars and of rockers, or jealous private denigration of the acting, demonstrate a wide irrelevance, a failure of thought as well as vocabulary. I begin to feel that the Berliners Brecht and Grass, and here Hollmann, to say nothing of

Gobert and Zadek, have done a great deal of damage, corrupting, as it were, a Shakespearean palate.

The Hamburg *Die Zeit*, likened in importance to *The Observer*, came back to the topic of the Festival, and to Howard in particular, three weeks later, in a powerful comparison between Howard and the American comedian Jango Edwards, 'two great entertainers': the latter appeared on the Reeperbahn. By picking on the facial and vocal mannerisms of Howard, and exaggerating the public's response to him alone ('He was celebrated as if he were a Messiah') in a way that might be considered grossly unfair to a Shakespearean company, the critic decided that Howard and Edwards could change places. Tricky stuff, I find, and very saddening. Has modern Germany *no* sense of a Shakespeare play whatsoever, so that one is not even recognized when it is seen?

Part of the reason for this may be an inability to comprehend any other way of doing things than the German way. There the subtleties of Shakespearean ambiguity are surgically removed under the anaesthetic of an outrageous 'concept' – 'a Hamlet in terror of the media' as in Cologne. When the full subtleties are presented for four hours in Jacobean English, which is technically modern but in fact very alien, a Hamburg audience, though proud of its excellent everyday English, is going to be heavily insulated from those central areas of uncertainty, of shading, of questioning that are to be found in a truly Shakespearean performance. Perhaps I have read too much German criticism and become over-solemn: but I am dismayed by the crudity and irrelevance, the fragmentary response, in the published reactions.

For one performance, the Thalia-Theater management very kindly arranged for my questionnaires to be distributed, and faithfully forwarded the completed forms to me later. As in Paris and Brussels, the questions were, with one exception, straightforward. I received one hundred and twenty-three replies. Just over half knew *Coriolanus* before they came to the theatre. Of those who knew it, two thirds name Schlegel-Tieck, seven Brecht and seven Hollmann as the translations or adaptations they had known – and one endearingly claimed only to have got as far as Act Two – no doubt the curtain then went up. Asked whether they found Shakespeare's language difficult, well over half said no, as one would expect in Hamburg, where English is pronounced not too differently from German. One commented 'No, wonderful to understand'. Just under half had never seen the RSC before, but sixty had seen one, two, three or four or even more RSC productions. One claimed 'one – this one last night'. The question about political orientation, to Left or Right, produced a consistent tone of rebuke to me for the irrelevance, not to say impertinence, of the question – even though Menenius, in Shakespeare's play, distinguishes 'us o'th'right-hand file' from the Tribunes (II.1.21–2). Sixteen said firmly that the production leaned to the Right, one adding 'Why not this way for once?' and thirteen thought it to the Left, one adding 'Because Coriolanus was seen critically'.

Caius Martius, warrior (Alan Howard).

The final question, asking for further comments, produced a flood of enthusiasm, in which two streams were clearly to be marked: a passionate hunger for more RSC productions in Hamburg, and an overwhelming preference for Shakespeare 'unchanged', 'something which is left in its classic context, not changed in order to reach an effect: Shakespeare does not need that' as one said. Another commented, 'This production shows me fundamentally why I go to the theatre. Its power of force and honesty made me very happy.' Though some remarks were slighter – 'Coriolanus is too cowboyish', 'His expression is too like Jimmy Carter' – there was evidence of a strong and steady thoughtfulness, worrying at the problem of balance a good deal of the time, bothered by an apparent lack of weight of effect against Howard, seeing Tribunes and Citizens as easily blown about, looking for 'characterisation' (my word, here) and not finding it, and puzzled. One spectator made the point that Shakespeare dismissed democracy, even though he himself did not know democracy as such, and knew only the human heart. Many were fascinated by the political manoeuvering: 'Coriolanus' low estimation of the people is certainly backed by the fact that even the Tribunes don't have the courage and the force to negotiate with him, but have to call for the patricians as middlemen.'

One questionnaire (typed, as were many) came back as a long, jointly-written essay about the performance, a profound consideration of Shakespeare in North Germany which made a plea for artistic purity, admitting that 'in spite of our great interest in theatre we cannot bear to see many more of the latest Hamburg Shakespeare productions (*Coriolan* at the Thalia, *Othello* and *The Winter's Tale* at the Schauspielhaus) which cause such dislike. The writers went on to make a fine point. 'What we hope from "theatre of the spoken word" (*Sprechtheater*) is above all that respect for the author and his work, that absolute faith in the work itself, which is nowadays self-evident in music: we want to draw our *own* parallels to the happenings of our time and our own personal experiences.' In the last paragraph of this essay the writers hoped that this production of *Coriolanus* 'would contribute to making future productions which *worked on* the central problems of mankind by means of Terror and Delight' – the constituent elements of Aristotle's *catharsis*, of course. The writers said they were interested in, and had gained from, the work of younger playwrights, but prayed that theatre directors would see the basic themes or problems of mankind as the older authors did. Two humble members of the Thalia audience, it seems, understood a little of what is in Shakespeare, and found it in our *Coriolanus*.

Though everyone agreed backstage that the Thalia technicians of all kinds had been superb, and though performances had been magnificent, some RSC people had wondered if all the tensions and conflicts and great, unusual, efforts had been worth it. It is not sentimental, I hope, to say that that essay on the back of one of my questionnaires shows that it was.

'Away, my disposition . . .' (scene 15); Volumnia (Maxine Audley), Coriolanus (Alan Howard).

Seven

Berlin

Just before the play began on Wednesday, 2 May, in a packed house at the Schiller-Theater, Berlin, I heard British and American senior-diplomat voices calling along the row behind me. 'I hope you've read it' said one, 'then you can tell me what it's about.' 'It's a tragedy,' said another. 'It's very simple. They all die.' I wanted to turn round and say to them, earnestly and embarrassingly, 'No, but you see, that's what's so fascinating about this one: they don't. All except one are alive at the end.' In the cleaner air of West Berlin it did seem that we were going to get to some of Shakespeare's terms at least.

That big Schiller audience, overwhelmingly German, watched and listened with profound attention: they sat very still, and feasted. Naturally acute and critical, some of the world's most sophisticated theatre-goers, they were not automatically to be pleased just with Shakespeare in English performed *con brio*. Terry's RSC *Henry 5*, with Alan and many of the present company, had been a sensation here in 1976: West Berliners, the press, television and radio had talked of little else.

That night, those I spoke to in the interval said that this *Coriolanus* production was altogether tighter, tauter, faster Shakespeare than they had seen elsewhere, and they were particularly overwhelmed by the power of the music. But their main concentration was on Caius Martius. They said they felt that this man was telling them that there was more to the conflicts than appeared – that he was saying to his mother 'I wish that you and I had not made it happen this way: I wish there had been something else that you and I could have done.'

This was Paul's second night as Menenius on the tour. Deeply as I missed Graham, I was impressed. Obviously in a few nights he could not build his own part as Graham had done over two years, but he was quick and sardonic, a less volatile patrician but one suddenly vulnerable, and a solidly tragic figure in his personal loss of Caius Martius.

The applause and curtain-calls were the longest we had had. Next day Frank Pauli in *Der Abend*, under the heading 'Hero with hot breath', gave a long, enthusiastic review. 'In the hands of the Royal Shakespeare Company the play blossoms into a poetic festival, a homage to their poet. The acting luxuriates in verse . . . A theatre-tradition with hot breath challenges our astonishment.' Pauli

Paul Imbusch as Menenius Agrippa

found music in all the speaking, and praised too the fluid rhythms of the visual spectacle. 'The production follows the poet's breath and the poet's heartbeat'. He was sensitive to Howard, who seemed 'created for one of the tiger-rôles in the art of acting'. He was the only critic to notice in print that Howard's Coriolanus had not only 'an assured self-consciousness when appearing in public' but that he had 'often a slight shyness when addressing himself to confidants'. He concluded, 'This is an evening of theatre such as is not to be found in companies in Germany, and not even to be imitated either. The English theatre, which has its own voice, here presents its best side. This is a guest-performance worth seeing and hearing.' Completely sold-out on the first night, the Schiller-Theater after that was beseiged for the rest of the week: to approach the building early on each evening was to be solicited a dozen times for a ticket, at any price, apparently.

We were received after the first night's performance at the British Ambassador's official Berlin residence in the American zone, in an unpretentious, friendly house, where big log fires and a general ease of atmosphere matched the welcome we were given. I found myself sitting next to an American Professor of Linguistics, whose name I knew; he was puzzled, and a little indignant, at inconsistencies in the pronunciation of Latin names in the evening's performance. I explained to him what Terry had done about that problem. At the very beginning of the rehearsal period he had written to four distinguished departments of classics in British universities asking for guidance. He had received four long, helpful and detailed replies, all contradictory. 'Whatever you do,' said Professor X, 'do not say "Volsky"'. Professor Y wrote, 'Above all, avoid "Volshy"'. Professor Z

Chief Stage Technician (Alistair Minnigin) and Electrician ('Jake', Derek Brain) talk with G.O.C. Berlin, Major-General R. F. Richardson.

admonished them not to pronounce it 'Volsey'. So Terry, Alan and the others went back to their original understanding, – that Shakespeare and his contemporaries anglicized foreign names as it suited them at the moment: Terry quoted a passage in *Pericles*, where within a dozen lines the rhythm demands that the heroine, Marina, be called 'Marinner' and then 'Mareena'. So here Caius Martius ('Ky-us Mar-shus') returned to Rome to be formally greeted as 'Kor-*eye*-o-lane-us', which softened, in his mother's later greeting, to '"Korryo-*lane*-us", must I call thee?' and so stayed. The American Professor was unconvinced.

At the reception, the Ambassador, Sir Oliver Wright, first sounded one of the notes which we were to hear throughout the time in Berlin – not so much a single note as an extended trumpet-call. He said to many of us at that reception that in some matters it was difficult for him to make a strong British presence: but 'one thing Britain is at the top in is theatre, and the RSC is at the top of that, and your coming to Berlin is the very best thing that could happen.' This was said to us repeatedly, by all kinds of people, in all our days there. There is no doubt that the condition of Britain in 1979 is often reported abroad very oddly indeed: my own experience in America, and now throughout Europe, within half a year, is full of examples of quite gross distortion in the press and in popular talk to make a widespread 'poor-Britain' syndrome. Yet there is great truth in the remark at that reception that, for Britain's image, one RSC visit is worth many Trade Fairs. I know, writing these words, how overwhelming is the European appreciation of the RSC, how huge the demand for more in the main European centres. Half a million pounds of British Government money, shall we say, to subsidise even short European tours by the RSC or a London orchestra like the LSO, would do, I know, so much to remove that scarcely-veiled continental sneer, that maddening assumed superiority of saying that they have worked for their success, unlike poor Britain, crippled, they assume you will agree, by tea-breaks. It is difficult for me to convey the astonishment, the exhilaration in a quite new experience, expressed to me again and again by younger Europeans on this tour, suddenly prepared to see Britain in a quite fresh light. Yet the bitter irony is that, writing these words, I have in front of me a notice from Stratford, sent to all the RSC Mailing-List subscribers, which says categorically that, under the policies of the new British Government, unless something is done quickly many of our theatres in Britain are threatened with closure, and the RSC itself may not survive. It seems that at the very top no-one either knows or cares. It is galling enough for actors – as one put it 'having been a star all over Europe, you next find yourself in the dole queue at Lisson Grove'. The current wider misapplication of money is about to do permanent damage to one of Britain's richest natural assets, the theatre.

The Number Two at the British Embassy in Germany is also a soldier in Berlin, and the diplomatic presence of the British Army was something most of us were happy to be aware of all that week in West Berlin. We had left Hamburg on an overcast, cold, wet morning. As it was May Day, and an official holiday through-out Europe, Hamburg airport had been deserted as well as chill. But the sun was shining in Berlin, and cheerful British troops met us with buses for us and a lorry for the luggage and took us quickly to the hotel.

On our first afternoon the Army showed us the Berlin Wall in all its depressing strangeness, opening a range of contrasting experiences we found to be the real

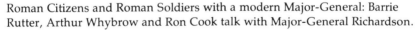

Roman Citizens and Roman Soldiers with a modern Major-General: Barrie Rutter, Arthur Whybrow and Ron Cook talk with Major-General Richardson.

Looking into East Berlin at Checkpoint Charlie.

mark of Berlin. The broad, central Strasse des 17 Juni, the continuation in the West of Unter den Linden, is wide and long enough for Hitler to have used it as a landing-strip for air-borne supplies in his last days, and it still has the empty feel of airfields. After seeing the sealed-off Brandenburger Tor and the Russian sentries at their war-memorial, with tank and guns, we were driven by long stretches of the triple Wall construction, so much still fronted with bricked-in shops and old doors of those first appalling days after 13 August 1961, and bearing from time to time the tarred wreaths which mark the deaths of would-be escapers. Road-signs still point to streets that are blocked off a few feet beyond them, only continuing hundreds of yards away after multiple impassable barriers in another world. We stood on a look-out platform, and gazed across an East Berlin waste to a bald mound, the sealed remains of Hitler's Bunker, and further round, Goebbels' Propaganda Ministry, Goering's Air Ministry, and (a building close to a tower-crane as if construction were still going on) the Headquarters of the Gestapo. Checkpoint Charlie had little custom while we were there: but the privately-run museum of pictures and objects connected with the wall and its personal effects was for a while full of RSC people. Later that day, Alistair was asked by the excellent Willi, chief of the Schiller back-stage staff, what the theatre had done to offend him as he was so silent and grim: Alistair explained that he was far from having any complaints about the theatre – he was simply brooding on what he had seen in the afternoon.

During that first performance in Berlin I had overheard a remark which to me became increasingly significant. At the point early in scene 16 where the Citizens had been brought in for their second official confrontation with Coriolanus – the dramatic movement which is to end with his enraged banishment of them – they stood in a close group and confusedly muttered among themselves while the Aedile tried to call them to order. An old man sitting near me suddenly said, out loud, to his wife *'Die Armen Berlins'* ('The poor of Berlin'). It seemed that in that picture of those doubtful, fearful faces, all those mouths opening in an almost Expressionist way, he had abruptly recognised Berlin since the war. I suddenly saw the other side of the *Wirkschaftswunder*, that high proportion of modern West Berlin which does not swing in the Kurfürstendamm or enjoy expense-accounts in the Kongresshalle, the old and the poor in an un-welfare State. For them Shakespeare shows flashes of sympathy, and I wondered where he saw such shattered citizenry, how he knew. Brooding on the old man's remark while troubled by the Wall, I thought a little bit more about Shakespeare's feelings for these economically trapped people of Rome. The citizens are fluid and volatile, untrustworthy, foolish, trying to swim with fins of lead and hew down oaks with rushes, at times utterly and criminally irresponsible, and yet deserving of pity, something about this play we have been slow to understand in the late twentieth-century West in our defensive need for artistic labels, for adaptations into familiar political stances. There was something elusive here, something Shakespearean in its intelligence and breadth of heart which even on my twentieth viewing of the play I had only just started to glimpse, and still could not formulate. Perhaps it took the extraordinary contrasts of West Berlin to make it even faintly visible.

The Tribunes look over the Berlin Wall into East Berlin; John Burgess and Oliver Ford-Davies.

On the glamorous Ernst-Reuter-Platz, with its clever fountains linked to the force of the wind so that on still days they were giant plumes and on blustery days small fat waterfalls, even at the foot of those smart tower-blocks, are found beggars: I am still astonished to be whined at with requests for money, as happened on several walks between the hotel and the theatre.

The contrasts were insistent. We were the first-ever occupants of the smart, big, not-quite-finished hotel. Apart from the disturbances of continual drilling from seven in the morning until five at night, and essential but inefficient lifts with minds of their own, we were comfortable, close both to the theatre and to the Kurfürstendamm. One could sit gluttonously for four hours or more at the Emperor-sized breakfast and lazily lounge and watch the German economy at work, men in steel helmets tidying, tidying, tidying as they went, devoted to work with discipline and cheerfulness, while smart-suited bow-tied men in raincoats carried briefcases and plans and got everything in order, making it correct and prosperous in this small island of wealth and excitement in the battered wasteland of the Eastern Zone. Ten minutes away was the 'K'damm' which, more than Hamburg or Amsterdam, seems now to be the permissive centre of the West. Some of the company, I'm told, sought exotic experiences amid the bold-eyed Berliners there; they did not tell me whether they had found

The RSC *Coriolanus* company at the Brandenburger Tor.

them. Several went to a splendid mixed sauna and emerged relaxed and glowing, having also seen rather more of their friends than usual.

Knowing my interest in Brecht, and especially his unfinished adaptation of *Coriolanus*, the two *Dramaturgen* at the Schiller, Herr Kerver and Frau Koch, urged me to visit the Berliner Ensemble in East Berlin, and indeed arranged by telephone for me to do so. Over a 'Berliner Weiss', a local drink so-called because it is either red or green, Hilary Bartlett of the British Council explained to me the procedure the day before. At the Freidrichstrasse station it was easier to cross the frontier than I had expected. At the theatre, I was efficiently received by the *Archivleiterin*, Frau Schloesser, and sat at a table in the Archiv room, and given the files and volumes to study. Here were most of the documents concerning the famous production of Brecht's play in 1964 by Manfred Wekwerth and Joachim Tenschert: and here in my hands too were those famous albums of photographs and text, the *Modellbuch* in which the production was recorded. It was unbelievable wealth for research, yet curiously dry and barren in its content.

Brecht worked on his version of *Coriolanus* at the end of his life, when he had been resident in East Berlin, his last home, for some years, beginning to build the Berliner Ensemble in the re-named theatre on the Schiffbauerdamm, where many of his earlier plays had been performed. The outsanding man or woman, whether in history or in fiction, is a familiar enough figure throughout his work and he had been interested in this play of Shakespeare since 1925. He frequently adapted Shakespeare and other British dramatists. Shakespeare in *Measure for Measure* gave him a basis for *Round Heads and Pointed Heads*; *Richard 3* for *Arturo Ui*: he had adapted *Hamlet* and *Measure for Measure* for radio in the early thirties and he recommends the casket-scene in *The Merchant of Venice* to set the tone in one scene of *Puntila*. He adapted Marlowe's *Edward 2* for the stage in 1924; Shaw's *St Joan* and Farquhar's *The Recruiting Officer* were altered to various purposes, and Gay, of course, gave him *The Three penny Opera*. His *Coriolanus* version is no butchery, and within its own limitations an interesting and indeed admirable play. It bears well the weight of application of his own often-quoted *dictum* that *'wir können den Shakespeare ändern, wenn wir ihn ändern können'*, a neat apophthegm to the effect that the ability to alter Shakespeare should match Shakespeare.

Brecht, for several decades said to be the single most important influence on European theatre, always thought of himself as doing something quite new. Though the celebrated theatrical technical terms – *Verfremdungseffekt* ('alienation effect'), *Gestus* ('gesture') and Epic Theatre, for example, become problematic when more closely examined, his techniques were, on stage, quite new, and at the time effective. Brecht was in revolt against bourgeois theatre. Early in the 1920s he wrote of his *Edward 2* production, 'We wished to make possible a production which would break with the Shakespearean tradition common to German

Ekkehard Schall as Coriolan in the Berliner Ensemble production of Brecht's version.

theatres: that lumpy monumental style which the Spiessbürger' [bourgeois Philistines] 'so love'. He found in Shakespeare's *Coriolanus*

. . . all these great and small conflicts thrown on the scene at once: the unrest of the starving plebeians together with the war against their neighbours the Volsci; the plebeians' hatred for Marcius, the people's enemy – together with his patriotism; the creation of the people's Tribunes – together with Marcius' appointment to a leading post in the war. How much of that do we get in the bourgeois theatre? (John Willett, *The Theatre of Bertolt Brecht* (1959) p. 122)

The techniques of harsh lighting, with the lamps visible, and of detaching the actor from his part, to give as it were a report on events, with cool, unemotional speaking, go right back to when Brecht was a *Dramaturg* in the Munich Kammerspiel in the 1920s, and were only really fully developed in the Berliner Ensemble. Such a theatrical manner was for a long time a matter of local public scandal, and first widely known only after performances in the late twenties of his first fully-developed attempt in Epic Theatre, the free adaptation of Gay into *The Threepenny Opera*. Germany has long had a tradition linking politics and theatre: it is a matter for discussion whether any political change there has been *caused* by theatre.

The impact of Brecht outside Germany came very late, and suggested that his greatness was more as a director, as a creator of unusual theatrical experiences, than either as a great dramatist or as a clear political thinker. In 1956, the year of *Look Back in Anger*, claimed in so many text-books as the moment of a rebirth of British theatre, and just after Brecht's death, the Berliner Ensemble visited the Palace Theatre, London for the first time. This occasion helped with the formation of the English Stage Company at the Royal Court, and pointed to the work of the Brechtian English playwright, John Arden. The second visit of the Berliner Ensemble to London in 1965 included *Coriolan*. That London experience of Brecht was to have a wider effect: some directors today recall the visits to England of the Moscow Arts Theatre and the Berliner Ensemble in the sixties as revelations, and the RSC style itself was even for a while slavishly imitative. Ronald Gray describes it:

At Stratford-upon-Avon the covered wagon of Mother Courage became a symbol of Brechtian intentions: a version of it was seen in *Henry V*, in *Coriolanus*, and even in *As You Like It*. During the same period it was usual to provide Stratford theatregoers with programmes containing historical facts about the figures Shakespeare wrote about, as though the plays were documentary and relevant to the times in which they were supposed to take place, or to the politics of the present day. (Ronald Gray, *Brecht: the Dramatist* (1976) p. 200)

Political theatre did not exist in England until the end of the nineteenth century, and there was little enough after that. What there has been in Britain, in the second half of the twentieth century is, one might say, entirely due to Brecht. In the United States, though his influence is well-known as an academic matter of cultural history, performance presents the dilemma posed by his theatrical intentions, for wealthy WASP college-drama-group activities are many miles from the

Ekkehard Schall as Coriolan.

factory-gates and the everyday workers' world. So too, it could be maintained, are comfortable audiences in traditionally bourgeois theatre-buildings of western Europe. It could be argued that his influence has been an illusion.

Brecht's *Coriolan* has not received the critical attention given, for example, to *Galileo*, *Arturo Ui*, *Schweyk*, or *Mother Courage*. This may be partly because he did not live to supervise its production, and partly, I believe, because it is thought to be so close to Shakespeare that it hardly merits separate treatment. Yet this is not so. Though not a mutilation, it is most distinctly altered into something quite other than Shakespeare – certainly in the text as Brecht left it, though Wekwerth and his team in their 1964 production made further changes which did in some ways bring it back to Shakespeare. It has been much performed: attendance figures for German theatre, West as well as East, show Brecht by far the most popular dramatist, after Shakespeare, and his *Coriolan* among those most performed. This play has the additional interest of having the words of the master attached, as it were, because, reproduced in several places, there exists a long *Studium* of Shakespeare's first scene, written, apparently before his play, as a preparatory dialogue between Brecht and three of his collaborators, and dated 1953. It seems that the work on the play which Brecht did finish was done between 1951 and 1953.

What is missing in the complete play MS is the work on Shakespeare's scenes four to ten of Act One, the battle at Corioles. The previous scene, the ladies at home, is shortened even before it finishes with Ithaca and the moths (line 84), and one more sentence (103–4). Then, in the *Complete Works*, comes Shakespeare translated by Dorothea Tieck, and a note that it was Brecht's intention to make one big battle-scene, a third scene for his first Act. He was to write this during production, and it would be effectively a record of positions and movements achieved in rehearsal.

This intention is characteristic of Brecht, who was able to command rehearsal-time unthinkable by British standards over as much as nine months, and something like a hundred full-day rehearsals, for one production. (Terry Hands' RSC *Coriolanus* was mounted completely in five weeks including two weeks' discussion: his three, uncut, *Parts* of *Henry 6*, seventy-nine scenes in all, in eleven weeks, all productions using actors engaged at the time elsewhere.) Brecht's *Coriolan* was first produced by Heinrich Koch at the Frankfurt Schauspielhaus on 22 September 1962, and at the Berliner Ensemble on 25 September 1964.

Working first from the text, rather than the *Modellbuch*, one notices three main areas of difference, though there are so many small changes all through that only a full parallel-text edition could hope to show the quite different colouring. Brecht's play is about one-third shorter than Shakespeare's. The first and most obvious change is in the role of the plebeians, now including from time to time The Man with the Child. The Citizens set the tone, both stylistically and politically – the two being not, of course, separable: thus, throughout, Shakespeare's poetry is either

Single combat between Coriolan and Audifius in the Berliner Ensemble production of Brecht's version.

removed or flattened, a dramatic phrase finding its consummation not in that sudden rich verbal intensity of multiple significance so characteristic of the Jacobeans, and of Shakespeare above all, but now in a theatrical action, the true Brechtian *Gestus*. Examples of this are everywhere, and make for something plainer, starker, almost grittier. At root it is a difference between a sort of mental luxuriance and a sort of political action, though I hesitate to make that difference more than very general. Brecht can himself import a striking image or two. For example, The Man with the Child is lower in the scale, and poorer, than the Citizens; they announce early on that they are going to get, by fighting, a better Rome for the Child, who is then asked if he will be brave when he gets no goatsmilk. Again, Menenius in his first longer speech, saying that the dearth comes from the gods and not from men, and that greater misery awaits the Citizens, adds *'So beisst der Säugling in die leere Brust / Der unglücklichen Mutter'* ('So the suckling bites the empty breast of the unhappy mother').

These Citizens in Brecht are altogether more rational, more knowing politically, more consciously involved in a class struggle, and quite humourless. Their Tribunes are their representatives, and have little separate existence; by heavy cutting, Brecht has removed almost all their initiative, their devious plotting and hypocrisy, and left them as mouthpieces for the politically active People, who know the economics of the corn-supply and act accordingly. When they hear that Coriolanus is marching on Rome towards the end of the play, they – far from attacking the Tribunes as in Shakespeare – decide to fight, and the Tribunes become leaders of the city when the patricians surrender. So strongly is the ideology at work that a few patricians join the proletariat for the coming struggle.

The second major change can now begin to be seen. Brecht has removed many of the individual marks of personality. The real force is the undifferentiated community, the People. Though he has imported a cobbler from *Julius Caesar*, and a Gardener, those sharp, comic signs of disunity and quirky fickleness in Shakespeare's citizens have disappeared. Though the shadowy and mysterious near-anonymity of the Volscian Adrian and the Roman spy Nicanor in Shakespeare have been replaced by a Rope-maker and a Tanner, the point in Brecht is their very lack of differentiation: workers are the same the world over, he is declaring, so instead of fighting each other they should unite in the common struggle against the patricians – or rather, as they actually say, enjoy peace, for war is a product of violent individualism, typified by Marcius.

The character of the hero of Brecht's play is flattened in many ways: by loss of poetry most obviously, and most subtly by loss of tragic significance. Brecht's play is not the tragedy of Individual Man; or rather, it is only that to show that the loss of such an individual is necessary for the forging of a new Rome. Here we are far from the shattered, debilitated, individual experiences of the survivors at the end of Shakespeare's play, where even the warrior Aufidius makes the last word of the play an appeal, 'Assist.' In Brecht, social revolution has taken place in the course of the play. Rome can now do without Marcius, and it is a much better place. The upheaval has been neatly characterised by an earth tremor which actually does remove 'yond coign o'th'Capitol, yond cornerstone'. Marcius is still central to Brecht's play (it is still properly named) but the shift is from the tragedy of an individual to the tragedy of a society that thinks it needs a dictatorial warrior-leader, and has to go through great suffering before it is rid of him. (There are those who see Brecht's play as a parable of the Hitler years.)

One incidental change in Brecht's text is the virtual removal of the force of Aufidius, and with him goes a puzzling range of possible dramatic meanings. Aufidius in Shakespeare is awkward and odd, absent for the whole centre of the play, but fascinating in his relationship with Martius. Aufidius' first scene (Shakespeare's Act One, scene two) is cut entirely, by Brecht, as is much else to do with him.

The third major change is simply that loss of possibility. Reading Brecht, one does not ask, 'What does it mean?'. Shakespeare's insight, we always feel, is ahead of us. Every year there appear learned books giving us definitive interpretations of the same Shakespeare play, all utterly different. That this is not likely with Brecht I can best illustrate by pointing to the plain message at the conclusion of his play. There, in the equivalent of Shakespeare's scene 24, Volumnia has virtually to ask the Tribunes' permission to go to her son: when she goes, her victory is one not of feeling, nor even of the *Gestus* of kneeling, and above all not caused by that hidden set of forces between mother and son only hinted at in Shakespeare in spite of the strong emotional speech. In Brecht, Volumnia wins simply because the smoke rising from Rome behind her will not be, as Marcius thinks, the sign of

The triumphal return of Coriolan in the Berliner Ensemble production of Brecht's version.

Rome's surrender, but coming from the People's forges as they make their weapons ready to defeat him. His tragic insight is only that he is replaceable by the People. His belief in his own supreme importance is destroyed. He is coldly killed. In a final scene in the Roman senate even a chill request for mourning is dismissed by Brutus, whose 'Rejected' is the last word of Brecht's play.

The *Modellbuch*, and other material, show some differences from this text. The great battle-scene, so memorable for all who saw it, did not follow Tieck, but used chanted names, some colloquialisms, and lines from more modern versions. Aufidius was restored to some importance, his duel with Marcius having truly epic stature, 'fought' as the programme put it 'on the backs of the poor people of Rome', an elevation again of the protagonists' individualism to show the dangers of society's dependence on such specialists: 'they must have their duel and it costs the world'. Some changes were also made to the Citizens, who began the play weak, worshipping Marcius as specialist soldier, and only gradually took on their political assurance. What was so startling to this reader of the documents about that production, sitting in the Berliner Ensemble *Archiv* on a showery day in May with his head full of Terry Hands' production, was just how many people there were on stage – seventeen Roman citizens, all with given Roman names: a further seventeen Roman soldiers, and thirteen Volscian soldiers. There was a little doubling, but I counted thirty-four such 'extras', as well as nineteen principals. Terry, also with nineteen principals, had nine 'extras', and still created an army.

Ekkehard Schall as Coriolan victorious in battle in the Berliner Ensemble
production of Brecht's version.

The *Modellbuch* is in three volumes, like very thick family albums, with photographs down one side of each page, the key phrase of the text typed against each
picture, and all keyed to Brecht's scene numbers. The first volume summarises
the seventeen scenes. The next is a complete account of the great Act One battle,
over a hundred and twenty photographs, diagrams and music directions: even
turning the pages and seeing all the stills was exciting; my notes record at one
point 'Full 13 × 2 line-up and charge. Thrilling mêlée.' The third volume records
all the Volumnia scenes in greater detail, with fine pictures of Helene Weigel, this
time even with a bit of lighting-contrast. In most of the pictures was the stocky
figure of Coriolanus, Ekkehard Schall. The *Modellbuch* showed clearly some
Brechtian devices: the huge, cinema-like title; the grand set – that magnificent
arch on its revolve; the flat lighting with almost no variation. The large groups
were expansively choreographed: Menenius told his fable of the belly to thirteen
citizens; Coriolanus' cry of 'I banish you' was to eighteen citizens, as well as
others.

I was also able to study much of Manfred Wekwerth's correspondence, and the
eighty-four page mimeographed document given, presumably, to everyone

involved, telling the history of the Coriolanus saga, an account of 'Shakespeare and his time', an anthology of comments from Schlegel to Lukács, and fourteen pages of Brecht on Shakespeare's first scene, the *Studium* again reproduced. Language-notes followed, and the thick document concluded with fourteen pages of 'First Memoranda towards the Conception 1963'. I thought of the few days of general discussion in Stratford in the summer of 1977, when not everyone had even been able to attend, before three weeks of rehearsal, and marvelled at the difference. Further documents outlined the music-cues, thirteen individual pieces, including scene 5, cue 11, *'Jubel ohne Chor'*; cue 12, *'Jubel mit Chor.'* – rejoicing without, and with, choir*.

During the hours I spent at the Berliner Ensemble I was able to meet a *Dramaturg*, Dr Scheller, who is an experienced adaptor of Shakespeare, having recently prepared a text of *Cymbeline*. He was surprised, indeed astonished, that we played *Coriolanus* uncut. In his experience two hours was about the limit for a German audience for Shakespeare. I was struck by how much of *Cymbeline* that work must leave on the editor's floor. I was also struck by how far apart are East and West: neither Dr Scheller nor I had any idea of what the other was doing. I did not know about current East German productions; he, though he had been in England seeing some theatre, did not know about the RSC's *Coriolanus*, nor even that it was playing a kilometer or so away at the Schiller.

Journal. Friday 4 May. Berlin. Also in the small room of the Archiv was Anna Cecchi from Rome, working on designs for her *Threepenny Opera* with the German composer Hans Werner Henze, which will open in Italy on the last day of July. Henze is this afternoon rehearsing and tomorrow performing with the Berlin Philharmonic. She will try to bring him to see *Coriolanus*. Anna and I came back to the West together: I thereby getting an Italian view of Brecht. Back in the West, below the station Am Zoo, I left her at a run, to catch our Army bus outside the hotel. As I scramble on, out of breath, I hear that the British General Election results are out, and flop into a seat no longer as a member of a mildly socialist State. Coming suddenly from East Berlin into such a free-enterprise West, I seem to have made a more than symbolic journey. The bus is taking us to a garden tea-party at the spacious residence of the British G.O.C. in Berlin, Major General R. F. Richardson, a quiet spot with wide lawns down to the Havel. After tea in the boat-house Pavilion, and a motor-boat trip, I am more than ever confused by the juxtapositions of the last ninety minutes, from the dusty emptiness of East Berlin streets, still with posters celebrating May Day, thanking the Soviet soldiers, from Brecht and his collective drama, even through emotional Italian eyes, to a Thatcherite Britain and extremely gracious German living among the highest British ranks.

Günter Grass is currently Germany's most celebrated writer, his novel *The Tin Drum*, now filmed, having sold nearly a million across the world. On 23 April 1964, for the Berlin quatercentenary celebrations of Shakespeare's birth, he gave

---

* For a number of points in this section I am indebted to Ladislaus Löb and Laurence Lerner, 'Views of Roman History: *Coriolanus* and *Coriolan*' in *Comparative Literature* (Oregon) XXIX, 1977, 35–53. I do not entirely agree with their conclusions.

an address to the Berlin Academy of Arts and Letters, in which he chose to compare Shakespeare's *Coriolanus* and Brecht's, and also to suggest a fine dramatic idea of his own. This printed address is very odd, not least in being full of strange errors like saying that Shakespeare wrote 'twenty-seven or twenty-eight, or perhaps only twenty-one plays' and that they may have been written by someone apparently called 'Sir Francis Bacon'. Yet in places Grass is quite interesting. He notes that the preface to his edition of Shakespeare says of *Coriolanus*: 'Because of its antidemocratic character, the play is seldom produced.' He admits 'I have never been privileged to see Shakespeare's *Coriolanus* on the stage', and he is almost willing to bet that no German producer will mount it in that 'Shakespeare year'. But the chief value in that address must be in the outline he gives of the play he was apparently already writing, which emerged as *Die Plebejer proben den Aufstand* ('The Plebeians Rehearse the Uprising') in 1966. The East German uprisings of 17 June 1953, so severely crushed by Russian tanks, happened on a day when Brecht was rehearsing. Grass has the fine idea of calling Brecht simply '*Der Chef*', and rearranging history to make him be rehearsing the first scene of *Coriolanus*. So there could be intense dramatic interest in the inter-action of the actors rehearsing a Roman insurrection while a real rising takes place in the streets outside and gradually impinges on the activity on the stage, focussing as relentlessly on what '*Der Chef*' will do as Shakespeare does on Coriolanus. It is a marvellous idea. The finished play (performed in English some years later by the RSC) is a little less than marvellous; though it has some interesting moments, it is a drama of missed opportunities. For one thing, the whole clever idea is sprung far too soon and there is nothing left to happen for the rest of the evening. That would not matter if '*Der Chef*', the thinly-disguised Brecht, had real dramatic life and interest. But that presented a problem for Grass, in that precisely how Brecht did respond to the real uprising is still something of a mystery. We know that he wrote a letter to the Central Committee of the Party, a letter which was doctored to appear in the press to look like abject conformity: but we know too that he, at that time one of the most honoured men in the DDR, with considerable power over public opinion, seemed to respond to the rising in no other way; he was certainly untouched afterwards. West Germany was deeply shocked by his apparent message of loyalty to the Party, and for a while would not perform his work. Brecht, after a little time of personal withdrawal, was soon back producing, able to move into the Schiffbauerdamm theater, modernized for him, and going to Moscow a year after that to receive the Stalin Peace Prize. So in a sense Grass has an insuperable problem with his hero. Though Grass is certainly sharp and alert to tricks of speech, he cannot handle the stage-masses in any way which will help him with his central figure, who in the end is treated with that kind of pitying, even patronising affection reserved, for example, by successful men for their old schoolmasters. Even the notion of the dilemma of the artist in society, making a conflation of Grass/Brecht/Shakespeare, is virtually untouched, and the antitheses between plebeians and actors, between Stalin-Atlee workers and actors, between plebeians and workers, between 'Der Chef' and Coriolanus, are muffled.

At the Schiller-Theater, Frau Koch gave me in a few moments of rapid emphatic German an account of the first night of this play, in that very theatre. The interest in West Berlin (and, more secretly, in the East) was very great, as it was all over West Germany, Switzerland, Northern and Western Europe. Seven television stations were present to cover the event. The queue for tickets stretched for over a mile. When West Germany's most celebrated writer opened a play about Germany's greatest playwright working with Shakespeare, the anticipatory excitement was so intense that one almost fainted. The evening, when it came, was by the same token as great a disappointment, for the play was simply dull. It would have been better, Frau Koch declared with animation, if it had been really, scandalously bad: but there was nothing to say, afterwards. It was 'mittel'.

That night, the strong, clear richness of Shakespeare's play of *Coriolanus*, uncut, un-doctored, performed with force and speed and exhilarating skill, came to me again after all this with the force of a clean, fresh wind from heaven. Those condensed, telescoped ideas, like 'Not unlike/Each way to better yours.' or 'his pupil age/Man-enter'd thus, he waxed like a sea' or 'let the pebbles on the hungry beach/Fillip the stars' came across like jewels: and Alan's power with the poetic passion of 'If you have writ your annals true, 'tis there/That like an eagle in a dove-cot, I/Flutter'd your Volscians in Corioles' was something to savour satisfyingly on tongue and lips and in the heart. Audiences, as each night passed in Berlin, responded more excitedly, and seemed to be living on their nerves to the ends of each of the spoken lines.

Journal. Berlin. Saturday 5 May. Disappointed that Anna, with or without her musical companion, had not made it to the play last night. But after breakfast this morning a phone call from her. Would I go with her this afternoon as joint guests of the Berliner Ensemble to see their *Mother Courage*? I explain that I have promised my younger son to see Berlin Zoo: so I spend two hours all alone in the cold Spring rain, with no-one else about, just me and the animals. Watching a keeper's tender talk while he is giving lunch to a very young gorilla I wonder whether, if all the apes in the world's zoos got together, they would have a language-problem: baby ape and adult man seem very close.

Anna and I cross the border very quickly, and have time the other side. We stroll down Unter den Linden, her umbrella as a silver-knobbed cane, over-elegant among the non-existent cafes and the vanished music, watched by the only other people in the wide street, East German policemen. I take her down to the other side, now, of the Brandeburger Tor, and standing by the pretty flowerbeds I show her – being myself by this time an expert – the Wall stretching away, so much tidier on this side. We study, walking back through the quite empty streets, other giant, red May Day posters hung on the buildings ('Vorwärts unter den Banner von Marx, Engels und Lenin') and try to understand the life we are seeing. An Intourist shop offers trips to Siberia, to Baikalsee, 'Die Blaue Perle Sibiriens'.

At the Berliner Ensemble we are guests, and conspicuous, though at first we don't realize that. I am astonished by the *gemütlichkeit* of the theatre; I suppose I had expected wooden benches, not the gold and velvet, the heavy decoration, the very comfortable plush seating. But the stage is the proper bare boards, with a massive and speedy revolve. It would be churlish not to like the performance very much indeed, though, it being Brecht, one cannot *warm* to it. The Cook is Ekkehard Schall himself, and Franziska Troegner is a fine Kattrin. Gisela May as Mother Courage seems to me magnificent. But I am as interested in the audience, young, a little restless, not unlike a schools matinée at Stratford. And therein lies something also unexpected: these young people have come to attend a classic, without any apparent engagement. The play is already a little bit fossilized, the audience more coughingly respectful than caught up: but again, perhaps that is just 'alienation' at work.

At the interval, Anna, scattering coats and open handbags, announces that she is very hungry. We decide that we are guests of the Kantine as well, and go down among the actors; the food is unfamiliar, and we settle for Weisskäse, and wait in the kitchen to have dollops of white stuff plonked on enormous plates. We sit a little apart from the costumed and made-up actors. We have much to say to each other about the performance, and are late back, and have to be put back through locked doors into the auditorium.

The second half brought me a moment of total astonishment. Just before Kattrin beats her drum on the roof, the two householders fall on their knees and say fragments of prayer – and the audience instantly broke into loud chattering. I had not fully realized what sitting in a good Communist audience meant, until that moment.

We ran through the rain from the theatre to the big glass building at the frontier-post. Anna is due back with Henze and the Berlin Phil, and we need to get through very quickly. But there are enormous queues. We wait, and are presently jammed into a body of close, odorous citizens: there is suddenly an unmistakeable atmosphere of fear, and a rough man in front of me micturates where he stands, all of us pressed around him. We shuffle forward, smellily. My passport, routinely taken for a moment, does not come back. The guard in his little box is holding it, telephoning. I am asked to stand aside. A higher officer comes. My passport is taken right away. Anna is through, and looks back at me stricken, on my behalf. I know there is nothing wrong with my passport, or with me, but I can't help a touch of fright. I tell her to go, as she can't keep them waiting at the Philharmonie. She plants both feet on the ground, holds up her chin, and says 'I don't go till you come'. In the distance, an even higher officer is summoned. I tell her, but myself as well, that bureaucracy being what it is, there is no relation between time passed and seriousness of situation. We cheerfully and slightly desperately discuss *Mother Courage*, a few feet apart, she in the West, me still in the East. Eventually, after a long time, my passport comes back down the line of officials, and, without a word, I am nodded through. 'Don't *run*', I hiss to Anna, and we force ourselves, not very successfully, to walk to the train.

That night, the RSC's last in Berlin, there was a fight at the Box Office over tickets, and a long queue for possible returns. Dr Bahn of the Schiller staff reckoned that in all about five hundred people were turned away. It was a remarkably still and sensitive audience, alive with expectation, rippling with response often at quite subtle moments, rising mercurially to Alan, making the evening a personal triumph for him especially, and at the end cheering the entire cast continually for a long time. Of all the audiences of the tour, that in Berlin was the most volatile, the most sophisticated: probably the hardest to please, but when delighted and moved the most generous in praise.

The Berlin press wrote at clever length, ultra-sophisticated, mannered, even neurotic. *Tagesspiegel* called its review 'Elegant and Erotic Power': the *Spandauer Volksblatt* 'Theatre Spectacle for a Blind and Deaf Audience'; and the *Berliner Morgenpost* 'The Great Fall of a Brilliant Stinker'. With such an English name Michael Stone in *Tagesspiegel* should have known better than to write of such a Jacobean play 'This must have been a pleasant tale in the ears of an Elizabethan audience, having Sir Walter Raleigh's sails before their very eyes.' He went on, 'Here, where Italian and German fascism is still alive in people's minds, such hardly-veiled praise for a tyrant is unbearable.' Stone suggests that Hands learned from the Berliner Ensemble's visit to London, and has improved on that – the RSC here 'emphasize their points with the same ritualistic style, which the Berliner Ensemble even on its best days staged in only a few examples'. He notes that as the Brechtian Caius Marcius, Ekkehard Schall is 'an actor of rather small stature' and his Aufidius was even smaller. Now Alan Howard, a foot taller than the plebeians who exile him, 'with every gesture and every sentence personifies the unbeatable and unapproachable hero. And Charles Dance as Aufidius is even taller still.' He goes on to call Howard 'a miracle of precision and forceful speaking,' seeing, even, his cultivation of 'the same staccato style which Brecht once introduced to the former Berliner Ensemble as *Verfremdungseffekt* . . .' (This seems to me to be more evidence of the absolute imprecision of that famous Brechtian slogan.) 'He is able to change his miming in the pauses between the single words and can achieve quite amazing effects. Again and again the audience is to see sudden transformations as visible processes . . . emotions are divided into their respective components.' He concludes, 'Whoever wants to hear the English language singing and rejoicing and shining, blustering and twittering, when it is performed by masters of the spoken word, should pick up a ticket . . .'

The notices demonstrated German difficulty with the Tribunes. For Stone they were, like the people, 'weak, cowardly, cunning and stupid'. For Hagmut Brockman in the *Spandauer Volksblatt* they were strong and manipulative. He sees the play that Shakespeare wrote as capable of many different interpretations, too, which is refreshing: but, failing to see what he expected (either satire or a drama of class-conflict), this critic is at a loss. He finds what the Germans always call '*Pathos*', the full expression of strong emotion, gets in the way, hindering understanding of the play as a 'timeless drama'. He finds various parts of the performance very impressive – the set, the choreography, the lighting: 'faces and situations and groups illuminated as living images in the manner of the darkened paintings of old masters, which reveal themselves without words. And for the 'blind' audience there are the corresponding effects in words: sound images,

"CORIOLANUS" FIGHT PLOT   cont.   SECOND PHASE.

Discard Left swords & grasp hands.

MARTIUS		T.AUFIDIUS
1).STEP RIGHT & CEDE QUINTE	←	VERT. CUT TO HEAD
2). " & CUT TO LEFT CHEEK	→	PARRY TIERCE
3). " THRU' & PARRY SEPTIME	←	CUT AT LEFT KNEE
4).BELLY SWEEP	→	WITHDRAW BELLY
ATTITUDE		
5)PULL ARM BACK	←	CIRCULAR CUT AT FOREARM
6).REPEAT STROKE TO T.A's ARM	→	PULL ARM BACK
7). ATTITUDE		
8).CUT TO HEAD	→	PARRY QUINTE
9).PARRY QUINTE	←	CUT TO HEAD
10).PARRY QUARTE	←	CUT TO LEFT CHEEK
11).MOLINELLO TO LEFT FLANK	→	BREAK DOWNSTAGE
12).SWAY BACK	←	BELLY SWEEP
13).MOLINELLO TO HEAD	→	MOVE THRU' TO S.R.
14). ATTITUDE		
15).ST. THRUST TO FACE	→	AVOID D/C
16).PARRY CEDE SESTA	←	VERT. CUT TO HEAD
17).VERT. CUT TO HEAD	→	CEDE PARRY QUINTE
18).PULL LEG BACK & AVOID	←	SWEEP TO LEFT LEG
19).BELLY SWEEP	→	AVOID & WRIST TWIST
20).TURN THRU & PARRY LOW	←	CUT LOW
21).REVERSE WRIST TWIST & CUT LOW	→	TURN & PARRY LOW
22).STEP & CUT TO HEAD	→	PARRY QUINTE
23).BEND BACK	←	PUSH TO CORPS A CORPS
24).PUSH AWAY	→	FALL BACK TO ARMS LENGTH
25).PULL ON TO EXTENDED ARM	→	LAST MOMENT PIVOT U/S
26).PARRY SEPTIME	←	SWING DOWNSTAGE & CUT LEFT HAMSTRING
27).WHIP THROW	→	SPIN U/S, FALL & LOSE SWORD.

Part of the Fight Plot by Ian McKay for the single combat between Caius
Martius and Tullus Aufidius, scene 8 of the RSC production

composed of full-steam *'Pathos'*, of pattering and cheery mood-music . . .' which includes the language. But Herr Brockmann does not know what to make of Alan Howard. 'Acting with astonishing energy and maybe deeply in love with himself, he presents quite a complicated Coriolanus; rolling his eyes, with quivering lips, parading like a peacock as if going to a Mr Universe competition, he modulates the text like an opera-aria . . . closer to opera-parody . . . *"Pathos"* and pose overrun the tragedy of the man Coriolanus and do not allow us to understand the symbolic meaning of his conflicts either.' Brockmann is lost, and almost has the honesty to admit it. He finds many beautiful moments, he says, and the three and a half hours is rarely boring: it is worthwhile encountering a well-cultivated national classic, but 'the mysterious play *Coriolanus* remains to be discovered'.

Under that peculiar reference to radiant skunks, the *Berliner Morgenpost* printed a long, scintillating account full of metaphysical conceits. Friedrich Luft writes disconcertingly: for example, 'Gloomy masonry, cement-like, occasionally cuts up the playing-area in Rome'. (*Cement? Masonry?* Was he perhaps in another theatre?) He begins by saying that 'English theatre-people, when playing their holy William, do not like to fuss about interpreting'. He notes that the play has a clear, definite meaning, and laments recent attempts to demolish that: here, he says, is the play itself, and you can take a slice of contemporary interpretation where you choose to cut (I paraphrase).

The notice focusess on Alan Howard, 'the tragedy belongs entirely to the protagonist'. 'The world of the drama only comes to a solution when this fascinating, this brilliant stinker of pathological self-confidence and suicidal conceit is fallen for ever'. Herr Luft builds a prose-poem of untranslatable words and phrases to catch the impact of Howard's performance: 'this super- and sub-human, this devil of self-conceit, this beaming figure of fire, dirt, defective love of mankind and tragic exaggerated pride . . .' Dazzled, Herr Luft finds the rest of the company 'far too weakly shaped'. Maxine Audley plays with forceful tones, but the part doesn't have the importance it did in the Brecht version. Indeed, there being no contrast in speech with Alan Howard, the rest is conventional and uninteresting. Howard 'remains the motor all through the evening', he plays 'a fascinating clinical case of a horribly exaggerated egotism. He plays the loveless man, who is deeply in love with himself, a brilliant monster, not even able to see his fellow men, to notice them, let alone love them from a distance'.

Eight

Munich

The company was in excellent spirits on arrival in Munich. The army had seen us smoothly to the airport in West Berlin, where a continual company ribaldry helped to disinfect the unpleasant, almost brutal security-checks on the way through to the departure-lounge – I would have described the guards as unfeeling, except that everyone was thoroughly frisked. (The West Germans were conducting a special search for terrorists that weekend.) The flight, in a richly built-up cloudscape, was bumpy and cheerful. In Munich the sun shone, the re-builders of the hotel were silent as it was Sunday, and the theatre was efficient and welcoming. Everyone felt that it was going to be a good stay.

Journal. Munich. Sunday. 4.00 p.m. I sit, alone and warm and comfortable, in the Café Arzmiller near the baroque Theatinerkirche, drinking Schokolade and eating a confection called Linzerschnitte. Exactly this time yesterday I was eating lumps of Weisskäse over blackening potatoes in the back-stage Kantine by the Schiffbauerdamm in East Berlin. Transition-blues have this time been swamped by culture-shock. Only an hour or so ago I was among the wearily all-knowing, good-looking, casually wealthy young people of West Berlin, and trying to cope with the inter-galactic prose style of the local theatre-critics. Now I am in an older world in every sense – around me is middle-aged, middle-class chic, in a town, in this part at least, of the middle ages. It feels pleasantly provincial. Older women come into the café in their winter Sunday best, having walked the clean precincts between the churches and looked into the prosperous, decently-closed shops.

The Senior Dramaturg of the Bayerisches Staatsschauspielhaus, Jörg-Dieter Haas, explained to me some of the history of the Residenz-theater in which we were playing. The 'Old Resi' was built between 1751 and 1753, a rococo building much loved in Munich. During the war, the whole interior was carefully dismantled and stored below ground in two halves a good distance apart. Between 2.00 pm and 2.30 pm on 18 March 1944 a daylight bombing raid on Munich destroyed the theatre, but not the stored furnishings and decorations. The 'New Resi', the present excellent building, seating 1050, was opened on the old site on 20 January 1951, the first theatre to be rebuilt in Germany. The ancient interior was then rehoused in a special building some distance away, the Cuvilliés, opened in 1958.

The three theatres that now make up the Bavarian National Theatre had only

The Residenz Theater, Munich.

had three productions of *Coriolanus* this century, one of them, a few years ago, the first Hollmann version, set in the nineteenth century, and not much liked. The 'New Resi' had only had nine English-language evenings since it opened, until our *Coriolanus* arrived, and six of those had been given by the RSC. The Residenz audience, Herr Haas explained, liked classical rather than modern theatre, though the same people as audience in the *Kammerspiel* down the road might like something very modern. Munich, he explained, still had the feeling of being the small provincial capital town it had been in the nineteenth century, even though it had grown in size and importance to rival West Berlin or Hamburg. Characteristically, though there is a theatre-going tradition, it is the Opera House which is loved. I began to see a situation more like Vienna than Hamburg, and found we were all looking forward to solid audience-response. What I heard of the four newspapers sounded promising for thoughtful, rather than ultra-smart, criticism.

The technical branch of the company was soon very happy. The unloading and get-in and building and lighting were done with unfussy efficiency – and the Kantine was found to be large, with fine food and cheerful service: Philip, walking among the tables in that big, vaulted area, said that if the RSC had that space anywhere they would instantly make four workshop theatres out of it. Basher reported that it was only the second theatre on the tour in which there had been time to check every lighting-state before the first night's performance.

Journal. Monday 7 May. Suddenly the sun is warm. We all need that. A lot of cheerful people gather in the Marienplatz to watch the Glockenspiel at eleven. We don't hear very much of the chimes, as one of the Sounds of Europe is going full blast: a pneumatic drill. German cities seem to be drilling themselves into a new, smarter order – rebuild the hotel! Sink another escalator! Deafen everyone! Don't let the RSC sleep! But further along, in a pedestrian precinct – and Munich is full of those – I am drawn by good flute-music, and in a doorway in the sunshine stands a girl playing Handel. That's better. That's the Munich of Mozart, Wagner and Strauss – even if its Handel, a British composer, as you must never call him in Germany. On the way back to the hotel I wait to cross a busy road. I brood on Little Green Men. New York doesn't have them: there the signs say 'DON'T WALK' as if going on 'OR I'LL SHOOT'. In Vienna they have absolute power: at 2 am. in the silence of a totally still and empty city, I saw a Viennese in a hat stand at a kerb, with not a car for miles, waiting for the Green Man before he could cross. In England the Green Men are gentlemen taking mild exercise. In East Berlin they have one leg sharply raised, eager to begin a Great Leap Forward, the Activists of International Pedestrianism.

Though I had been told that the theatre was 93 per cent sold out, it was very far from full for our first night, and many people left at the main interval. And though there had been advance newspaper coverage, there were neither posters nor pictures to be seen anywhere in Munich – a circumstance that by now was depressingly familiar. Such audience as there was, however, was deeply attentive, shocked into close attention, I felt by the power of Shakespeare – except, that is, for a pair of young men in the circle, who increasingly found tragic moments comic and openly laughed at the wrong places, finding some of Alan's later effects distinctly hilarious. Then as the applause was building at the end, these two opened their lungs and booed, very loudly. They aimed the boos at Alan. The rest of the audience, stirred by this, responded with passionate applause, against them. They booed the more, and went on booing till the curtain-calls were over.

That night at the reception for the RSC, given by the theatre, we heard a good deal about the local phenomenon of precision-booing as a theatre-habit, apparently well-known in Munich, especially at the Opera. It was explained to us that the young men were probably opposed to such mannered playing, to such great 'Pathos' and were themselves very probably actors, and jealous of Alan. If it was political, then it must, people said, be from the left-wing, a response to making a 'a right-wing dictator so attractive and so wonderful.'

Professor Herta Renk of the University of Eichstätt, commenting to me on the frequency of booing at the Opera, where every single performer could be singled out, let alone a star tenor, and where rival opinions can lead to booing-battles, went on to defend the custom as keeping everyone alive: indeed, she developed a theory of the value of *Skandal* in German theatre, where classical acting can be dead, formal, and lifeless, so that a director who creates a scandal is provoking signs of life.

Journal. Tuesday 8 May. A day off. *Coriolanus* and the RSC can go hang. I go by train to Tübingen in Württemburg – a long way. I spent a post-graduate year in the University there after Oxford, a quarter of a century ago, and it calls. So on a warm, clear day I ride through wide dandelion-filled fields and patches of woodland approaching the edges of the Black Forest. There are neat, gabled, red-tiled houses everywhere with daffodils and tulips. Pretty wooded valleys remind me of Vermont. Spring has come at last along the Neckar. In the small town I find a small hotel and stay the night. Next morning, visiting my old room in the Evangelisches Stift, I am recognised by the porter and remembered. On the long railway journeys in spite of trains running late the acerbic manner of railway ticket-inspectors and guards was pleasant after so many toothy smiles from air-line cabin staff.

Gordon had organised a bus into the mountains. Most of the company went, and relished the sunshine and the sights. They visited the fairy-tale castle of King Ludwig of Bavaria, Neuschwanstein, and the unbelievable baroque church at Wies, calling also at Oberammergau. Everyone who went told me, with especial emphasis, that it had been a really superb *company* day, hugely enjoyed together. As Alan later commented, taking a show like that on tour needed much more free time: and as it was, the actors never got to see other plays.

The second performance was to a packed house, sold right out, and received with rapture – no boos at all. The third, and last, Munich performance was to an exceptionally alert house with special delight for Alan's vocal play with the 'Voices' speech, and concluding with even greater and longer applause.

I talked to David Shaw-Parker, actor, writer and conversationalist. While others of the company are quickly sampling the local scene, which close to the theatre in Munich means a range from the Hofbräuhaus with its hearty music and heartier drinking to the Schloss Nymphenburg, the art galleries or the English garden, DSP gets on with his novel, on some days achieving in thousands of words written what a full-time, copper-bottomed descendent of Trollope or Balzac would envy. He described his novel to me as like a mixture of *King Lear* and *La Condition Humaine*. Conversations with DSP are sharp-cornered affairs, occurring themselves, I found, at the sharper corners of travelling experience. Thus, waiting outside the theatre in the Max-Joseph-platz I found DSP perched amid late Baroque elegance in the afternoon sun. The meeting felt like something from *Alice in Wonderland*.

Earlier I had talked to a puzzled Jill, who had been offered various parts after the tour and couldn't decide which to take. She had been faintly distressed by a diplomat at one of the recent receptions who had tried to sympathise with her for having such a 'mopey' part in *Coriolanus*, when she was trying to get across something else altogether. Jill felt that it was very important that Virgilia, through her silences, communicated several vital qualities: his mother had chosen her, she felt, thinking she was a mousey little thing, but as usual in those cases the mother chose 'wrongly' in choosing 'rightly'. Jill was convinced that Virgilia and Caius Martius had a fabulous sex-life, a 'terrific thing going' that they shared and had no need for speech about. She said that Virgilia knew from the beginning that her husband was going to die: she doesn't sing. Throughout the play she has a different 'voice', a silence-voice, as it were.

We talked about the words 'O the gods!' at Act Four, scene one, line 37, just before her husband's departure. The Folio text, the only contemporary one, assigns the words to Coriolanus. Alan and she had felt that it didn't fit in with him at that point. It certainly matched all her similar remarks, from the very

David Shaw-Parker in the Max-Joseph-Platz, Munich.

beginning, 'O Jupiter, no blood!' and so on; she says 'O heavens! O heavens!' just a line or two before.

It is, she said, a difficult part, as throughout she has very little to say. The pleading scene in which she has nothing to do but register the entire time is very exhausting. Alan, she reported, was always a great help, 'giving one hundred per cent on the stage, even if you've both got your backs to the audience – and you respond to it.' It is, she said, a desolate ending for her. Quite apart from it being sad, she knows that his mother will go on working with that little boy; she, his widow, will just fade – and as Graham had put it, she is for ever going to have to listen to that woman raging about the house.

The *Süddeutsche Zeitung* printed a fifteen-hundred word essay by the senior Bavarian critic, Joachim Kaiser, entitled 'Was this *Coriolanus* old-fashioned?' He began by suggesting that Peter Zadek 'with his bloody hands' might have been present at the first night, because the house, after all that stage-fighting, turned itself into a battle between 'vehement applause' and 'persistent boos'. Kaiser gave the first half of his notice to a careful account of the excellence of Shakespeare's play, how he piled matter on matter, adding 'even more immense aspects' to it, culminating in the fickleness of the crowd. 'For Shakespeare even all that was not enough. I remember well how after World War II in *Coriolanus* performances the emigrants who had just come home, embittered and love-sick, felt with horror, and understood, an outcast who wanted to take revenge on his native country, his former fatherland, but could not do so: for also the homeland is a great mother, with the sweet pain of a mother-tie.'

But from that point on, Kaiser expressed great disappointment. There was, he announced, no 'conception' (*'Auffassung'*) none of the famous English interpretative unmasking-cult (*'Entkleidungs-Kult'*). Instead of 'private' speaking, there was highly-coloured recitation, anti-psychological tendencies, a delight in spectacular, strongly physical, Punch-and-Judy effects, which all led to self-satisfied banality. Yet though this Coriolanus was 'not written by Brecht, hardly by Freud, nor a history Professor named Schiller', the further, greater, attitudes and delights were simply not there. Kaiser found the staging to be like open-air opera. It would be impossible, he claimed, for those without sufficient English to understand more than just a simple Wheel-of-Fortune tragedy. Alan Howard demonstrated contrariness, shouting to show himself mild, and so on. Kaiser, in the most ponderous, finger-wagging words, found even the humour no warrant for the company failing to realise a serious, exact piece of theatre (*'wahrhaft ernstes, genaues, interpretierendes Theater'*). He concluded with the information that English theatre is in a state of major crisis. One of the really great, world-famous, Shakespeare companies had this *Coriolanus* on its programme: it was annoying to him not that it was old-fashioned, but that it was so unimportant, so like an alibi for something not there, so unserious, (*'so ungewichtig, so alibihaft, ja so un-ernst'*).

Both the *Abend Zeitung* and *Münchner Merkur* noted that Brecht, and Hollmann, had turned Shakespeare's play into an anti-war, anti-hero, pro-plebeian piece, and therefore RSC's reading was for post-war Germans, sensational. In a fizzy, slangy, trendy notice, Armin Eichholz, in *Münchner Merkur*, though hearing sounds beyond the threshold of audibility, like the supposed pronunciation of Rome as 'Harrouma' described it as 'a great triumph' because it gave what German directors never did – strong attitudes, shattering speech, an assault on the audience. It was much better in its direct theatricality than anything done by German directors, still going on with tired old alienation-effects. The diction was glorious, pompous, uncompromising. 'This production can best be summed up in Howard/Coriolanus' words, "I play the man I am". This is what we want. We may well envy the company being allowed to mount such a production. And we vow never to read another programme-note to Shakespeare.' George Salmony in *Abend Zeitung*, also contrasting the Berliner Ensemble and Hollmann, said that the RSC played the tragedy straight – 'naive, elementary, brutal and horrific – which it is'. 'They articulate cleanly and precisely. . . . Alan Howard is an actor of the kind we need more of – hard to pin down in his mixture of straight histrionics and many-faceted eccentricities' (*'schwer zu fassen, zu deuten, einzuordnen in seiner geradezu chaotischen Zusammensetzung von gradlinig konventionellem Histrionentum und pluralistischem Aus-der-Reihe-Springen.'*)

Rolf May in *TZ München* began 'For the first twenty minutes or so the production alienated more than it delighted, for we in Germany are no longer used to

Early in a get-out: dismantling a high musicians' gantry.

such unbroken classical *Pathos* . . . Every word and sentence is relished as a melody; single consonants are exploded like trumpet-blasts. Howard presents a war-hero of breathtaking presence.'

I talked to Charles Dance about Tullus Aufidius. He was conscious of the mystery of the man, and related him to Hotspur, in that so much of him was in a state of mutual admiration with an enemy in many ways like himself, as Hotspur was to Hal, and he was similarly full of unexpected responses. 'That after so many times that they had met and fought, after he had been humiliated by his own men, after his furious speech in scene 10 explaining to what lengths he would go in his hatred, then to greet him and invite him in for a cup of tea is incredible.' I suggested that this world of the Volscians with its conspirators and assassination belonged to the Rome of *Julius Caesar*. Though we agreed that there was no warrant for making the Volscians into noble savages, as had so often recently been done, Charlie did not agree that Aufidius was a politician, nor that he was a waning fighter, as we knew Alan felt. He was wary of any political explanation, feeling him driven by jealousy of 'the worst and most dangerous kind, that driven by love, because his hatred for Caius Martius is so great that it might as well be love. Jealousy may hate so vehemently that it can turn to love. – that is the kind of jealousy that makes men mad, the driving force of ambition, as in *Macbeth*.' He felt that Aufidius' last words maintained that meaning – '"He shall have a noble memory" – unlike me.' He is blaming Caius Martius for what he made him do, revealing his hatred and jealousy.

Herr Haas kindly arranged for my questionnaires to be distributed. The audience at the 'Resi' provided me with the fullest and liveliest answers. Many were typed, and I am grateful to all those people who wrote so much, and so well.

Nearly half had not seen the RSC before. The question asking whether *Coriolanus* was known before produced a picture of Munich doing its homework, almost all having read it, mostly in Dorothea Tieck; but eighteen had read it in English, and several more bi-lingually. One commented that no copies of the text had been obtainable in Munich for many days – 'which must be taken as a good mark for Munich.' One-third said they did find the language of the play difficult to understand but with qualification in every case, such as only up to the first interval, or only when the actors spoke very quickly, or only occasionally: the rest categorically did not find it hard, adding such notes as 'It was so clearly spoken that even I could understand.' One answer shall be translated in full: 'No! I found the language of the play wonderful, easy to understand, and expressively pronounced. If it were up to me, Shakespearean English would still be spoken today.'

My question about detecting a political tendency produced not so much answers as indignant outbursts. An equal number felt a leaning to the Left and to the Right, in both cases strongly qualified. The rest, at length, with vehemence, and giving reasons, denounced the question as unworthy of Shakespeare, or of great

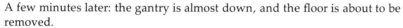

A few minutes later: the gantry is almost down, and the floor is about to be removed.

Soon after, a wall-section goes out.

art, or of the production, or just unworthy – though one, having pointed out the wide range of human sympathy in the play, did add that it was of course the '*Royal* Shakespeare . . .'. There was a lot of good, sharp observation, some wit. One writer, in answer to my either/ or question, said simply 'Jein' – that is, 'yes and no'; and one asked in reply 'Is the *Iliad* Social Democrat or Christian Union?' But such outlines do not give any proper idea of the clicking of tongues my question caused, the sorrowful rebukes spelled out, or the adjectival variations on 'What a stupid question!' I do not, however, hang my head too low. All my correspondents are right, of course – I mean 'correct' – in their indignation, and their very force shows how far the RSC performance was from stock German responses to the play as too anti-democratic to play, or so obviously polarised that all Brecht, or anyone, had to do was to polish the glass a little.

Similarly, the final invitation for further comment produced uninhibitedly strong reactions. One, having answered the 'political' question with 'Can't say: left after 45 minutes', added as further comment 'Bad, over-loaded, not credible, conceited. Poor Shakespeare!' Another wrote: 'Production even more disappointing than *Henry 5*. It relies on the smallest possible combination of effects for effects' sake. Over-simple basis of certain costumes, ''choreography of symmetry'' and opera-like lime-light.' Another found the production 'not entirely adequate to the meaning of the play': the hero 'played around too much', the mother was too weak 'to give the right features to the mother-son relationship in the framework of the tragedy.' One found too much '*Pathos*', too much of 'a show' towards the end 'whereas Shakespeare emphasises the word'. The costumes and set worried several: 'What does blackness – or is it spacelessness – mean?' 'The costumes of the three main groups didn't hang together.' Two writers took more leisure to expand their views: one, who had not known the play before, felt it was a very dry, difficult, play, full of obstacles, and too long for a guest performance. It lacked proportion and contrast among the parts. 'Only Alan Howard emerges from the actors, . . . his brilliance and self-indulgence, mixed with irony, and the fact that he does not take anything seriously, are hardly to be borne.' For that writer, the best RSC play was *The Royal Hunt of the Sun*, – but 'the Old Vic company was even better.' Similarly, the second asked 'Why must Mr Howard above all ceaselessly shout in this singing, crying, declamatory style? Always posed a-straddle, always energetically (and mostly unmotivatedly) throwing around his head, never allowed to get down to the softer notes. That all seemed to me too superficial . . . the constant declamation, the almost entire lack of psychological interpretation, and the higher stylisation made me tired . . . I lost interest: it didn't give me any insight into the play and the *dramatis personae*.'

Several took the opportunity to correct the impression given by Kaiser, the *Süddeutsche Zeitung* critic. 'His comment was incredible and dishonest.' 'The criticism by Kaiser was not adequate . . .'. 'The Munich critic, himself fixed on the theatre of yesterday, calls *this* old-fashioned, and asks for depth and psychology!' Several, too, tried to account for the first-night boos – it did seem that quite a few in Munich saw the play more than once – and there was a stream of more detailed

One of the big moving walls is now down and being dismantled —

— as its ribs are removed.

appreciation of set, costumes, music and the parts outside Coriolanus and Volumnia – the Tribunes here came in for praise: 'Fantastic Tribunes!' one interjected
in the middle of discussing something else. The full flood of comment is strongly
appreciative, without that cascade of superlatives from, say, Vienna. Almost all
the replies say 'It was wonderful, please come again' in one way or another. A
dozen or so develop this far more fully, valuing the fact that there are 'no violating
interpretations'. That, and 'the will to make the language as a language of art into
the central experience, and the incomparable *élan* of the actors – all of them – these
are virtues which are not often to be found on the German stage and never in such
a concentration'. 'What a pity that we don't have theatre like that in Germany:
over here only Zadek and Co. have all the say.' 'One is indeed grateful in
Germany, where many plays are only misused as an alibi for childish gags
(Peymann, Zadek) . . .' Several noted with gratitude that playing the original
does not impede the spectator with 'interpretations', adding 'outstanding speaking and directing. Recommended for copy in Germany'. One comment is of
particular value: 'For a German audience, used in the past few years to seeing
Shakespeare as a modern *polit-drama*, with actors in jeans and street-clothes, and
the action in a kitchen or a slaughter-house, these straightforward theatrical
effects are at first somewhat strange, almost old-fashioned, even nearly comic. I
was involuntarily reminded of cinema in the thirties, an art of acting which for the
present-day spectator has something of the ridiculous. The character of
Coriolanus however, is tragic indeed, and Alan Howard performed very well . . .

but one of the difficult things for the spectator is that the play doesn't offer any object of identification at all . . .' ''Good'' characters for whose fate we could care do not appear, besides the ''pale'' Virgilia.'

Finally, from all the comments, themselves worthy of far more treatment than there is room for here, I select one as most characteristic: 'A very interesting production which we will talk about for a long time. Everyone was stirred but people thought of it differently (*Sie hat die Gemüter erregt und die Geister geschieden!*)'.

Uniquely in Munich, one member of the audience took the trouble to write to me, three weeks after we left, a long letter – three thousand words – explaining her own reactions, and those of many friends. She had talked to a lot of people, and found that a great deal of the play had been taken in at depth: they were all shocked by Kaiser ('I myself had thought that he understood a bit more about literature . . .') She hoped the English don't understand enough German to comprehend this 'disgrace to our culture,' and envies England, its critics prepared right from the start to admit that their opinion is subjective. For her – supported by her researches – the strength of the production lay in its almost oratorio-like outer simplicity (*'der fast oratorienhaften äussern Kargheit'*) which reminded her of Wieland Wagner. She admired the set and its clear, crisp use, especially at points like

As floor-sections are lifted, a lighting-bar is stripped of lanterns.

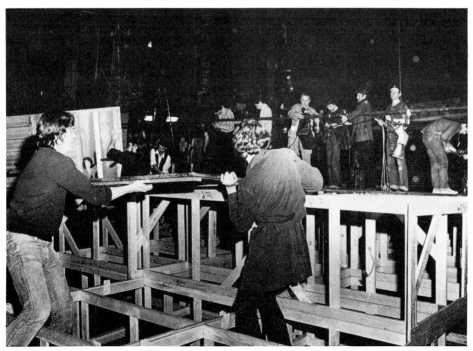

the battle-scenes where Shakespeare's action is almost too demanding. 'I could imagine some German director using different means, trying to point up the decadence of Roman society with a jet-setting Valeria . . .' She noted that the RSC use of language had led to controversy, but says that for her the antiquated feel to the language only illuminated the distance from Shakespeare's time to ancient Rome, adding 'strangely enough, the old-fashioned German in Schlegel-Tieck disturbs me more.'

A very musical correspondent, she went on to praise highly the richness of nuances in the voices of each single actor, conveying with the minimum of action the maximum of characterisation ('Herr Kaiser doesn't seem to have noticed anything of that'). She found 'breathtaking' the use of key words like 'custom', 'honour', 'market-place', 'love' (even in the plural) and 'peace', and how they changed through the differentiations made by various actors, above all by Alan Howard ('the legitimate successor to Olivier'). She lamented Kaiser's failure to understand, or notice, the reason for Howard's vocal range in places, 'reaching the limit of what can be borne, in order to show the boredom of the sophistication in which Coriolanus is brought up, including the boredom with himself.' She was acute on the pain of aristocratic Volumnia and her son's lack of interest in privileges, or even the fruits of his being a war-hero (*Kriegsheldentum*), rejecting this greatest Roman virtue not out of despair, Howard showed, but as the chance result of his upbringing and education, 'which, besides a morbid tendency to sophistication, couldn't offer him anything else.' She saw a very wide range of suggestiveness in much of Howard's acting, and even in the Senate 'a latent and strong sympathy for those creatures, the plebs, seems to come through; they are narrowed by custom like him, even if on the other side . . ., "I love them as they weigh"'. (Alan commented that he felt a connection between himself and the plebeians, whose coarser speaking he understood better than the sophisticated, compromising, educated speech of the Tribunes, for example.) In Act Three scene one 'it is not that he despises the people, but that he starts to open their eyes to their true position, after having held the mirror up to the nobles; 'what should the people do with these bald Tribunes?' That seals his fate. 'His death is demanded when he reveals himself as a traitorous innovator to whom everything is suspicious or respectively dangerous.' She went on 'I think this is a crucial point of Terry Hands' and Alan Howard's interpretation; it is clarified by the inexorable, deep-drilling, breath-stopping expression on Howard's face when he measures the faces of the aristocrats and plebeians alike in the Senate, and so closes the circle, challenging those spectators one by one as he goes along the stage.' Whoever is not made breathless by that short scene has yet to experience 'I talk of you' as a monologue, a dialogue with the spectators (Act Three, scene two), 'which is simply overwhelming. From this point on everything rolls in its right sequence.'

Nine

Zürich

The independent Swiss do things differently, we found. Their undemonstrative, wealthy city had excellent posters everywhere advertising *Coriolanus*, so that wherever you looked you saw a big, first-act, sardonic Alan.

The theatre we were to play in, however, was not in the centre of Zürich at all, but out at Oerlikon, on a small corner of a trade-exhibition complex, a multi-purpose building like a community-hall, miles from where people live, lost in a weekday-business region, a long tram-ride from the lake. When I first went there, there seemed to be no-one at all to be found connected with that theatre. Someone from the RSC said, 'I've met the stage-staff. Rather unpleasant, I found him.' Indeed, when Basher had arrived the day before, he had found that this gentleman had not hired any of the additional lamps which had been arranged, and he had had to spend much of his first day cruising Zürich in a taxi picking them up. The reason, he was told, was that in Zürich 'people are not interested in the lighting, in the set, in the costumes – just Alan Howard.' The whole thing had the air of being run by a Town Hall committee which met only occasionally – a fairly accurate impression, it turned out. The good lighting board had not long been installed; Garry had to teach the operator how to use it. The imported stage-crew was inexperienced but enthusiastic. Alistair won a battle to hang black drapes over at least the upper part of the windows – there was to be a matinée on Sunday. Since he was not allowed to put them inside, he by-passed the regulations and spent hours on the roof hanging them outside. The dressing-room situation was not good. Fifteen actors had to share a 'dressing-room' containing nothing but round café tables and chairs, without basins, mirrors or adequate lights. The band were jammed in the first aid room, stage management, technicians and wardrobe in a tiny dressing-room.

There was much disillusionment, too, in the fact that the hotel was on the other side of the city, two long tram-rides away; and, of course, it was being rebuilt: the pneumatic drills started promptly at seven every morning. When, finally, for the first night's performance, the hall was found to be only two-thirds full, it did seem that the tour was going to fizzle out rather than end.

Yet by the time the Company went back across the city to the hotel in the small hours, four things had happened to help *morale*. Terry had arrived, to stay with us for the rest of the time. Within the first five minutes the audience was hugely appreciative and reacting quickly; when an insensitive woman in high heels clattered her way to her front-row seat five minutes after the start, to get the full force of Alan's first 'What's the *matter?*' aimed straight at her, the response of the house was joyous, and stayed high. Then at the end, as the first full curtain-call was taken, when the whole cast stepped forward in line, a cascade of huge flowers began from above the stage, showering the cast and the set with colour, going on and on until, smiling, astonished, and delighted, the actors found themselves wading through petals ankle-deep. They began to throw the tulips and chrysanthemums forward for the standing audience. It was a totally unexpected welcome, and deeply appreciated. After the show there was a reception in what seemed like a large committee-room, with much good food and wine, and speeches of welcome. The British ambassador, Mr Alan Rothnie, who had come specially from Berne, said that Zürichers knew the British had the best actors in the world – and the RSC was the best of the British. The Secretary of the Swiss English Society made a courteous speech of welcome in faultless English. The Mayor of Zürich, Dr Wittmer, explained the city's policy of bringing foreign-language, especially English, theatre to their city. So that he could bring the RSC again often, he hoped that the pound would continue its progress – downward. Alan replied, in a neat speech, admitting they were helped by 'a hell of a good script-writer'.

Talking that evening with local people, I realised that though Zürich, with many less than four hundred thousand inhabitants, is by far the smallest city we visited, it has nevertheless a historic and still-thriving theatre-interest. The city is proud of having given a home to great writers: Joyce, of course, had written much of *Ulysses* there: and the Zürich Comedy Club, the English amateur theatre which he founded, still thrives. During the second world war Zürich welcomed refugees from Hitler's Germany: Frisch and Dürrenmatt both gave plays to the city. In 1938 Brecht himself was there, working on *Arturo Ui*.

Journal. Bahnhofstrasse. Zürich. Saturday 12 May. I gaze at a fragment of the moon's surface, on display in a Bank window, part of a big sequence on our galaxy. This little bit of dirty rock, beyond value in exotic significance and cost to retrieve, is nicely symbolic of a city where every other building does seem to be a jewellers when it is not a bank. It takes a day or so to get your eye in to the wealth. Something else took a while to register: suddenly there are chestnuts in full bloom by the lake: we are in the warm south. It is hazy, however, so I cannot see an Alp: I feel cheated. That is unlike the efficient Swiss. Cosmopolitan Zürichers tell you that everything works, which is pleasant, but that it is difficult to be an eccentric; to park a car six inches over a line is to risk a note from a neighbour. I wonder how they would take Caius Martius.

Something that everybody says on this rapid tour is 'When we were in – where was it . . .?' So, recently, only a few days ago, in – where was it? – I talked, separately, to Oliver Ford-Davies and to John Burgess about the Tribunes. Oliver,

The Tribunes: Sicinius Velutus (John Burgess) and Junius Brutus (Oliver Ford-Davies).

himself once a history don in a Scottish University, plays Junius Brutus with careful passion, thinking, planning, politicking, knowing what arguments to marshall. He reminds the citizens that the history of 'the noble house o' th' Martians' included 'Publius and Quintus . . . that our best water brought by conduits hither' – there is, I find, more than a touch of the early Fabian Society about Junius Brutus. Sicinius Velutus, by contrast, shorter, stockier, is the bull-dog to Brutus' proctor, his feelings less under his own control, probably the more dangerous of the two.

Both actors agreed, separately, that Terry had set his face against making them 'character' parts, rich with accents and elaborate characterisations. John had not been at the earliest Tribunes rehearsals (he took over from Tim Wylton at the end of the Stratford run having been Second Senator till then) and Oliver had been playing in *As You Like It* and so had not been able to get even to the earliest discussions. But they were clear that Terry from the first wasn't thinking of them as typed, one as the north-country one, the other the cheeky cockney, or what-ever. He wanted their own voices, and for them to explore the parts and see what happened. They both felt that the five tribunes whom we hear have been appointed are taken from a mixture of people in public positions – a doctor, a magistrate, a trades-union leader, two people from the boiler-room whose force-ful opinions are known and who can be trusted – a cross-section of a middle-class with roots in a working-class. Of course, to have built a 'character' in the strong tradition of English acting, and kept it fresh, would have been easier: to root it in themselves was very demanding. (I noticed that Oliver and John went every-where on the tour together. In the same way, the Citizenry tended to separate themselves as a group and root about for cheaper digs in each city, all the Volscians seemed to be loners, and Alan kept himself very much apart – all this apparently being unlike what happened to the 'band of brothers' on the *Henry 5* tour.) After he took the part over, John received a note from Terry, telling him not to characterise too much, 'to trust the text, and the text will reveal the character'. Oliver thought of Brutus as having, in modern terms, been a lecturer at a Polytechnic, possibly got rid of for being too left-wing, who had also gone into local politics and become a magistrate; this was his first salaried job since he had lost his last one. Having once thought of that, Oliver was for forgetting such background and 'just doing the text'.

There was no doubt to me that this spareness, so revealing and indeed moving, as I found it, puzzled most European audiences, who couldn't understand why Alan Howard had no tremendously-developed reaction – the modern catch-phrase would be 'feedback' – from these two, especially as the Tribunes were usually most violently altered in the more familiar re-written versions in Germany.

In this production they carried a stream of development in the play not usually understood. Far from leading a Popular Front, the Tribunes are usually in difficul-ties, are often quite undecided, and at the end have achieved nothing. Brecht made them take over the armed city against the threat from Coriolanus with the Volscians, and there Brutus, we recall, had the last word, as final and almost as curt as a Soviet '*niet*'. As Oliver and John explored Shakespeare's play they found no rôle for themselves in Rome: being neither patricians nor plebeians, they had to make their own place, and were constantly at a loss what to do next. So they found that the edges of the parts were blurred in a way that was wholly valuable. They were the only group to have no music or special sound to mark them. At the twenty-fifth viewing indeed, I suddenly saw a glimpse of a new country of meaning in them, how their strange, elliptical unfinished syntax represents a difficulty in doing any kind of talking at all – Sicinius' 'Be-mock the modest moon' is in Gothic script, as it were; he is trying to talk up to his level of new office with patrician ease, and he can't keep it up for more than four words. Again, the Tribunes were only happiest with lists and papers to read from, legal-sounding phrases to declare, or – in Brutus' case – a bit of history to expound, or journalist's colour to make a short feature out of, as in that piece filed on the spot, datelined Rome, in which Brutus describes the local scene at the reception of the victorious Martius in scene eleven. Their occasional speaking in unison (marked so in Shakespeare's text) and their speaking at other times very diversely, illuminates this; as does also Menenius' description of them in the first scene of Act Two (scene 11). At first sight, it seems that Menenius is giving a quick, coloured character-sketch of them, and we may take it at face value. But he is in fact describing his own inability to grasp them ('you are a pair of strange ones'). Menenius, it can be argued, has the shrewdest political mind of the play: but even he cannot get the hang of the Tribunes.

Their costumes admirably displayed the difficulties Rome had in fitting them into its system: an off-white gown, an anonymous jacket, boots, a little hat with a hint of revolutionary cockade – a concocted 'uniform' of bits and pieces. When they first come on, these clothes are new and awkward and they don't like the hats. By act three the hats are firmly on, and their comfort with their clothes makes a statement about bureaucracy. At the end, Brutus (who has been seriously roughed-up by the mob, off-stage) comes back gown-less, tattered, his white muffler hanging loose, giving a down-and-out effect.

They are often left alone on stage at the end of a scene of activity, standing still and apart. This characteristic profoundly puzzled many in Germany to whom I spoke, one intelligent theatre-goer in Hamburg becoming quite vehement about the Tribunes being 'mere dolls in a window'. Both actors, on the other hand, said separately to me that as off-stage, at their deepest moments of concentration they were still, so on-stage, in times of thought, they felt they should be motionless. I feel that a further explanation of the German difficulty here may be that the language that Shakespeare has given to the Tribunes is of an unusual special difficulty. Coriolanus speaks rich, dense, metaphor. Menenius speaks sharp, patrician, table-talk. Volumnia, the Italian hero's mother, has operatic solo-arias. But the Tribunes speak a scrap-book of tried-out styles, with newspaper-cuttings pasted in, and useful texts of scripture, and even a page from the Demagogue's Manual. This must have been exceptionally hard for non-native English speakers to follow, especially because it is not obvious that it is hard, because the vocabulary appears to be reasonably straight-forward. So such stillness, representing that so much of the time they were in the process of thinking things through, must have also deprived audiences – who were already at sea because the Tribunes were not the familiar caricatures – of a range of physical mannerisms and gestures, however slight, which might have assisted their understanding of the difficult speech.

John also pointed out the variations in speed; that sometimes they have to think very quickly, conditions forcing very rapid decisions on to them. They occasionally get breathing-spaces, but mostly events are moving extremely rapidly, and so the stillness of intense concentration was more natural to them. This also made clear two other remarkable effects: when Sicinius loses control and throws himself upon Coriolanus in scene 14 he has been swept away by feeling, and shows what happens when he acts without any thought at all. 'He has become so incensed and outraged,' said John, 'by what he sees as the utter despotic intolerance and intemperance of this man that he loses himself, and actually attacks him, which he certainly wouldn't do in his right mind, because

Coriolanus is three times the size and a great fighting machine. The idea of the little enraged man throwing himself upon this man-mountain doesn't accord with Sicinius' intelligence. At that point his emotion has taken over. Junius Brutus, even at the times when he's very angry indeed, always retains some form of control.' Sicinius has been betrayed by his own nature, not being able to cope with the speed of events, not giving him time to think. (A small amount of re-assignment of the speeches had slightly strengthened these individual characteristics.)

Both actors felt that at the end of the play Shakespeare, wanting to focus on his central figure even more than he has done, and to consummate the tragedy, has only time to suggest in a sort of short-hand what happens to the Tribunes. Their 'It cannot be . . .' in scene 22 is a mere sketch because Shakespeare has a lot of other ground to cover: similarly, Brutus' 'half my wealth' at the end of that scene, Oliver felt, was only a hint of a suggestion that he has done well out of his office; accepted back-handers, possibly been corrupted. Even if that is forcing the word 'wealth', there is no doubt that they have both disintegrated by this time. 'Part of the problem,' said Oliver,' is that there isn't a proper pay-off to the Tribunes. Shakespeare loses his need for them, and only sketches them in in the last Act, and so doesn't allow much room to explore the way that power, as I believe, has corrupted them; and now they haven't anticipated trouble and they don't believe it and can't cope with it.'

With a different kind of ellipsis, they both found, Shakespeare in the middle of the play gives no clue why the Tribunes suddenly decided to banish Coriolanus when they had seemed set to arrange for him to be killed. Apparently even up to his entry in scene 16 they are still going 'to break his neck'. 'At various times,' Oliver said, 'they announce what they're going to do and then you don't see them doing it. Shakespeare is very brilliant with the Tribunes politically; he constantly keeps the balance between their being shrewd operators who appear to have a plan and stick to it, and being swept along by events, changing their minds, not operating their plan. When they announce, for example, that they are going to manipulate the people, and then the people completely let them down and almost to a man allow Coriolanus to be consul, then they say "that's finished, we don't see any way out of that", even having harangued them. Then it is one of the *people* who says, "well, we'll just break the rules". Shakespeare is such an ambivalent writer that you can read that as a manipulated suggestion. But it seemed to John and to me not to be. We constantly feel that they are at the same time both manipulative and reactive.' Similarly, Brutus, Oliver felt, seems to have two conflicting characteristics. 'When you first see him he is absolutely right with a word like "devour" – "the present wars devour him" – that is a remarkable word, the part Caius Martius is playing does "devour" you. But when he explains to Sicinius that he accepted second-in-command because as everyone knows in that position the buck doesn't stop with you, then he is totally unjustified in his reading. He is saying "I understand that completely; that is how you manoeuvre for power" which is absolutely wrong for Caius Martius. Again, in scene 22, when he's asked to sum him up, Brutus gets him right as "a worthy officer in the war", as "insolent, o'ercome with pride", but then when he goes on to say "ambitious past all belief", I don't think that in Brutus' terms Caius Martius *was* "ambitious past all belief."'

So Shakespeare, both actors felt, kept two things going at once with the Tribunes: shrewd political judgements, and an absolute failure to understand – particularly, of course, to understand Caius Martius. This, I feel, gives a further sense of their unreality in this world of Rome. Caius Martius is the central subject in Rome, the matter of all men's analysis: but the Tribunes are out of key, painted in the wrong colour, on a different wavelength – one is left only with metaphors to describe their uncertain location in the Roman scene.

I asked about their place in the Senate in scene 12 which Terry presented very much as a Parliament on the Westminster model. John described their unease on first entering 'like a new Labour member from Barrow-in-Furness at his first entry into the great Gothic portals of the Houses of Parliament. He might be partly overawed and partly truculent. They are partly attempting to do the right thing and partly attempting to do their own thing, getting very bored with Cominius when he goes off on long interminable eulogising about the feats of Coriolanus.

> Cominus (Bernard Brown) eulogises Coriolanus in the Senate: Menenius (Paul Imbusch), First Roman Senator (Mike Hall), Junius Brutus (Oliver Ford-Davies).

And then of course they begin to realise that the patricians are not united: they are anxious, there is apprehension: Cominius has been badly affected by the whole experience, and is worried about Coriolanus, and he doesn't see him as a states-man but as a fighting machine. Menenius stops him and says with strong emphasis "he is right *noble*". So then we wait, knowing from what Cominius has revealed, and from our own observation, that Coriolanus is going to blow it, and we are going to see that he does: and there might even be a split in the Senate so that they have to find someone-else to stand, some-one less dangerous.'

I myself came only slowly to realise that one reason for the shadowy figures who haunt this play, like 'our late dictator' in this scene, could be to suggest alternative possibilities, that multiple richness of available meanings which is the mark of the greatest art, and is so antiseptically cleaned off the surface by Brecht, and so totally burned off and the ground sterilised, by Hollmann. The opening speeches of the Senate scene indeed indicate that three are standing for consul-ship, just as there are in all five Tribunes appointed, and very many groups of plebeians. Some modern thinking about the play has tried to deny such open-ness, to fix a single view-point. We were all three in agreement that it was irrelevant to claim, for instance, as some writers and even scholars had done, that with the Citizens and Tribunes Shakespeare was in this play expressing alarm at the domestic situation in Jacobean England. Günter Grass, for example, a romancer rather than a scholar, painted a lurid picture in his 1964 Berlin lecture of events giving Shakespeare 'first-hand knowlege of what we today call the class-struggle.' Grass knows to his own satisfaction that Caius Martius is modelled on Raleigh. He makes other, even wilder, assumptions about English history and 'this bothersome play, in which Rome's plebeians, like London's artisans, are cowardly rats and ignorant dogs, in which Roman patricians, like English nobles, are noble lords and heroes without taint.' Grass's remarks, influential in Europe, have not unfortunately been understood to be the unhistorical private imaginings that they are: and Grass is not alone. Even usually judicious scholars make unwarranted historical parallels. Certainly, provincial disturbances did occur in England in 1597 and again ten years later. But drawing these specific parallels to *Coriolanus* comes from a misunderstanding of the wider suggestiveness of that play, and among much else misses the difference between city and country in the first decade of the seventeenth century. Shakespeare's city of Rome is full of volatile *citizens*. It is a city play. There is no question of anything outside Rome at all – or even that one way out of the problem would be to decamp into the country, as happens in both Shakespeare's sources, and in Brecht.

Shakespeare always hints at multiplicity. Just as he sketches in a larger number of Citizens in their city tribes than we ever see, so he suggests a more fickle relationship between the people and their Tribunes than has often been assumed. The biggest damage Brecht did was to make these two men dominant at the end. In Shakespeare, they are left with nothing clear, not even martyrdom. The official has simply descended to the level of the Citizen, as indicated by the Messenger's retort (given here to First Citizen) 'Sir, we have all/Great cause to give great thanks.'

John summed up: 'We don't get killed because there is not a lot of point in killing us. We've simply outlived our usefulness. The play is so very much a concentration on the dilemma of an individual and a society embodied in one man, the only one who dies. Terry's production illuminates and accentuates that. Whatever catharsis is in the play has to come from the blood-letting from this person, this symbol, this concentration of so many things. Everyone's preoccupations, hopes, plans, desires, concerns are in that one man, and therefore the Armageddon, nuclear explosion, or whatever, is built up to the final resolution within the boundaries of that one personality. He is the centre of the wheel. About myself, I know only that I am diminished. My standing with the people I've fought for and represented is absolutely on the floor. They want to have nothing at all to do with me. I'm rejected by the people and by my fellow-Tribunes – and I've never had any kind of communication with anybody else but them. I have nothing left but anonymity.'

Journal. Zürich. Sunday 13 May. A morning at the Kunsthaus admiring both the building and its contents, especially the super-Romantic Shakespearean paintings of Fuseli – the three witches, Titania and the fairies with Bottom, Falstaff in the laundry-basket, 'Perdita asleep before her house with view of the forest and the three fairies' – *there's* a fine Romantic imagination, bettering Shakespeare with a vengeance. Yesterday I saw the Chagall windows in the Fraumünsterkirche, and passed by the strange frescoes in the cloister below. I had been driven through Küsnacht, golden in afternoon sun off the lake, passing the hidden place where G.G. Jung lived and worked. Undemonstrative Zürich may be, but I have been in closer touch here with greater movements of a venturing spirit, up to the surface of the moon, down to apparently limitless depths of the human unconscious, than in all the more flamboyant cities we have visited on this tour.

At the time of the Sunday afternoon matinée the sun shone very warmly, and lake and mountain and fresh air must have called to most Swiss. The heavy black cloth which Alistair had rigged outside the hall was some help, but sitting in such a not-fully-blacked-out hall on a bright, warm afternoon on those hard chairs in their rows gave an irresistible impression of a quite different context. As the applause finished at the end of that matinée more than one person present expected the Headmaster to mount the stage at the front and congratulate a rather more than usually accomplished Sixth Form on their Speech Day Play and would the prefects please stay behind to supervise the stacking of the chairs? Though the hall was only half full, the young, informal audience was eager in response and sat with that special stillness we had found with all good continental audiences. I found myself seeing many things freshly: the crossing movements of the Citizens' staves, and how their pattern threatens Menenius: that the Waiting Gentle-woman, (Deirdra Morris) standing for some time after her one-line announcement in scene 3, ethereal in her strongly side-lit presence: the fresco effect of noble figures in a space, throughout. I had not seen so clearly the two vertical pillars of light at the back of the set nor heard some details of the orchestration of some of Ian Kellam's music. The audience found new comedy in Alan's victorious greeting of his mother 'You have, I know, petition'd *all* the gods/For my prosperity,' and there was a sudden rustle of excitement on his scene 15 'I will not do it.' For all the last hour that audience sat exceptionally still, lost in wonder, as far as I could tell. I was struck afresh by all the tricks of repetition of tiny phrases, like 'I'th'city of kites and crows' and 'thwack our general', 'They are rising,' and of course, supremely, 'Boy!' Repetitions occur all over Shakespeare, most remarkably in *Hamlet*: but in this play, seen that afternoon, they became freshly insistent, demanding explanation – or at least a lot more thought.

That evening's performance was the last. Not just the last in Zürich, nor the last on the tour, but the last. The stage crews would return to Stratford or the Aldwych. The set and costumes would go into store. The actors would scatter tomorrow from Heathrow, some across the world: a few had work to go to, most had not. Whether everything would ever assemble again for this play was quite unknown. Few plays are revived when they have already run for two years, but it is not unheard of, and, as we noticed, it is something that tends to happen to a Terry Hands production.

The last performance was good, the audience matching any we have had. Watching, and noting the impact of the play, still so fresh, I recalled talking to people all over Europe, many of them actors in great theatres, who had said 'Why can't *we* do that?'

The Company gathered after the show at one end of the committee room. The management stood everyone a glass of wine. There had been, throughout the day, a rising sense of company togetherness, which now found expression in a cheerful, low-key, very short, party.

Terry stood in the centre and spoke. As they had been the beginning, so his words were the end of two years of *Coriolanus*. He reminded us of the British debt to European theatre in the previous decade when they had stimulated so much useful debate, particularly the Berliner Ensemble and the Moscow Arts Theatre. Perhaps, he said, that was the essence of what we should do – cause debates. This European tour had been one way of returning those visits. Taking this play to Europe had been one of the most dangerous things they could have done. It was such a flinty text. It was long. It was very concentrated. It was, in addition, political dynamite, increasingly made so by the fact that Brecht and other versions were very well-known. Live music had not yet been rediscovered on the stages of Europe; nor had live actors. The text demanded co-ordination of mind. It is not permitted in the modern European theatre tradition for a play to come out upon the audience. When it does, as *Coriolanus* did, it is dangerous.

The reaction of audiences and press had been triumphant, he noted, especially in Berlin. There has been one bad review, in Munich. He had expected far more. Audiences and press alike had responded to the fact that we were making a statement, showing respect for the author, for the actors and for the audiences. It had taken a great deal of courage to make that statement, and to do it with that kind of energy.

He thanked the technical staff. He congratulated them on coping with unfamiliar theatres, languages and dialects, saying that they did most noticeably seem to thrive on it – every time he met Alistair and Neil they seemed bigger. He thanked the musicians, who started them off each evening with that direct drive right into the emotional heart of the play, and who had had to cut short their performances in the foyers because the audience were staying to listen to them and not going in. In thanking the actors he pointed to one peculiar thing about the British system. Our actors are very good, and it is something that we take a pride in, and something that is noticed throughout the world. Yet if you tell some of the people we play to, many of whom are actors themselves, while we are going out with such a flourish, that the actors are going back to England now to the worst job security in the world, they don't believe it. Yet actors are still going to go on tour, with the RSC, with a play like *Coriolanus*. He commended each one for a decision made entirely personally, a decision made not for the RSC but for themselves, individually. The RSC was proud to be associated with that effort, with what they had achieved for themselves as actors throughout Europe. He did notice that many of the '*Henry 5* lot' did in fact return to work with the RSC.

'That is the end of *Coriolanus*,' he said. 'Well, we ended *Merry Wives* in Japan, in Nagoya, in 1970, and that came back. We ended *Henry 5* in England, in Bristol, in 1976, and that came back. Now we end *Coriolanus* in Switzerland, in Zürich, in 1979 . . .'

Ten

'Coriolanus' in performance

The demands of the part of Caius Martius are unusual. The physical athleticism needed, the overwhelming command of the entire theatre at every moment, and the absorption of so much unredeemed hatred are obvious. Less obvious is the necessity, as Alan Howard made the part, to be a high-energy motor for the whole three-and-a-half hours of performance – sometimes to a European first-night house more interested in the social rather than the theatrical occasion, which must have been rather like trying to race across a ploughed field.

There are, inevitably, capillary actions between part and actor. Henry the Fifth's excited discovery, as Howard played him, is that he is one of a band of English brothers, victorious in Europe: I heard a lot about how the *Henry 5* tour was very much a close fellowship. *Coriolanus* by contrast is a play in which no-one talks of anything else but that man, his separation from the rest, yet the dependence of everyone on him. This 'lonely dragon in his fen' who is never for a moment ignored, or let be – the man who leaves wife and home and friends to join an enemy, horribly nurturing a cutting remoteness – all this is not shrugged off in the wings, especially not past midnight in an alien city with restaurants closing. The giant size of that Roman warrior, distant from any comfortably normal world, could be difficult for an actor to live with day after day. It was the more understandable that Howard, this time, tended to keep himself rather apart from everybody else when not on stage. This, existing there in real life, is what Hands and Howard saw as the heart of the play – the problem of the person of special powers, needed by a society for success, yet not containable by it. Though the society does not even half begin to understand him, he has to be accommodated somehow, however awkwardly.

One way of doing this is to make a special label, 'the finest actor', 'Caius Martius Coriolanus'. The play seems endlessly to work at this, conjuring with a constellation of notions about labels and names, Caius Martius' extra name being itself the title of the play. For example, beyond the more straightforward references, in a Roman play, to Hercules or Mars, Jupiter or Tarquin, there is indecision about what ordinary Romans should be called – are they Citizens or Plebeians? The play says both. Again, are the aristocrats nobles, patricians or senators? How do these differ? The play uses all three terms. There are shadowy

Caius Martius' wife Virgilia (Jill Baker) listens to his mother Volumnia (Maxine Audley).

figures like Cotus or Publicola, living like meteors in half a line, never seen. Less invisible but still puzzling people like Adrian and Nicanor solemnly exchange names. Aufidius fails to recognise Caius Martius until he hears his name. Twenty-five lines after Martius has received his own new name, Coriolanus, he forgets the name of his host in Corioles. Yet almost everyone in the play receives special forms of address, right from Virgilia, who is 'my gracious silence', to the citizens as 'you rotten cry of curs', from a Tribune as 'Triton of the minnows', to Caius Martius as 'boy of tears'. And so on. In their earliest discussions, Hands and Howard and the company felt that the giving of names raises, rather than solves, difficulties. Why are the ladies all 'V's? Volumnia, Virgilia and Valeria are all in Shakespeare's sources, but they are still puzzling. Why do they match the Volsces, who themselves have a name that can sound like 'voices' anyway?

Trying to make a link between given title and expected action was a matter that I found, watching those performances, increasingly demanding attention. Safely distanced in Corioles, Caius Martius' incredible power and skill could be felt by Rome as a sort of ideal, what a perfect Roman aristocrat should be: first a super-human fighter, then a wise policy-maker, then a good father to his people. But the essence of an ideal is that it should be quite unreal, because reality is problematical. It is most unlikely that a tremendous fighting-machine will have the first idea about civil policy, or even how to get on with his fellow-men – the Pattons and MacArthurs of this world cause trouble as a full-time occupation. The man who widows and unchilds other people as his special expertise is not necessarily going to be very paternalistic. And the foolish patricians of Rome decide to make this conqueror of far-off cities a consul of Rome itself. It is a lunatic decision, for his very name indicates that he doesn't belong at home: in so naming him, they show that they don't want him.

His importance as a distanced figure of unreality, however, is stated very early on, long before the events at Corioles. His mother's first speech is a complex, intimate confession of Spartan brutality. Making a fantasy of herself as his wife, she then prefers his absence getting honour to his presence in bed showing love. Her vision of her son at work a few moments later ends, after a perversion of beauty, with a line of distancing irony:

> The breasts of Hecuba
> When she did suckle Hector, look'd not lovelier
> Than Hector's forehead when it spit forth blood
> At Grecian sword contemning. Tell Valeria
> We are fit to bid her welcome.

That whole bloody vision in verse is accompanied by the presence, in Hands' production, of something else almost unreal, a visionary angel, the Gentlewoman standing behind illuminated in young, feminine beauty. Again Cominius' long account in the Senate of Martius' youthful exploit is full of strange, 'unreal', counterpoints. One does not need to go so far as some modern American critics and see there a brutish sexuality – that is to over-simplify: but certainly Cominius' praising 'voice' is complicatedly ambivalent. On the battle-field, Cominius has been fulsome in praise; here in the Senate, the fantasy about Coriolanus is gross and horrifying – a matter excellently shown by the triple giant shadow of the warrior standing apart. Ideal figures are complex, disturbing double-natured things, and the further they are off the better: as soon as they are brought close, they show alarmingly problematical characteristics. There is a mis-match at the heart of the play: things are wrong, in the wrong places, out of kilter. Even the Senate meeting is not proper, but an 'after-meeting'. All is not by any means happy among the patricians. No wonder the Tribunes in this production were so frequently so much at a loss.

This developing bewilderment, the sense of the play's mysterious sensitivity to the unexpected, characterised the production. Strong and forceful as the story was, playing the full text with such full voice also demonstrated that the play at its heart expresses doubt, a characteristic of not knowing what is going on, of being unable to find central truths. Coriolanus, sickened by the result of Rome's attempt to elevate him out of his real world, goes off to 'a world elsewhere' which we never in fact see – an unattainable ideal. When we see him again, he has arrived at a place so like Rome as to be its twin, where he is again instantly elevated to god-like position. Just like the common people in Rome, Aufidius' servants switch from

Aufidius (Charles Dance), defeated, with his Volscian soldiers.

one set of feelings about Coriolanus to another while they watch their superiors patch together fantasies about each other. That 'world elsewhere' turns out to be only a populated fantasy. Leaving Rome, in scene 17, Howard was relaxed, even comfortable; sorry to leave his family and friends, and for a moment imagining that he could take them with him; but, really, glad to go from the impossible strains of being the ideal Roman in an ideal Rome, neither of which existed in any kind of reality. Caius Martius, approaching the stature of a tragic hero, does not see himself going to any more normal place of refuge (when he next meets his wife, he is specific, for example, that he has not been with another woman) but he now understands that he will exist in another fantasy, both his own and Rome's, this time without the power to harm, as a lonely dragon. A dragon, however, is what the Volscians want, and the tragic process of trying to fuse together the ideal and the real happens all over again. Menenius' later description of him is as a fabulous beast:

When he walks, he moves like an engine and the ground shrinks before his treading.
He is able to pierce a corslet with his eye, talks like a knell and his hum is a battery.

He has now become a creature entirely of Rome's fantasy, and altogether safer at a distance than he was being full of treasons in Rome.

The great movement from fantasy to reality is what occupies the later part of the play. It is a movement which involves the whole illusion of drama, the part the audience has to play in the celebration of tragedy. Again and again in this production I was conscious of an underlying understanding about how fantasies worked. Twice, Howard described a slow arrival of his mother from far up-stage while he himself stood right forward looking deep into the audience. His mother, it seemed, was so much a living inner figure for him that her materialisation did not need his real eyes. Again, the accounts of events frequently did not match what we had seen; for example, Coriolanus told Aufidius that he had sent Menenius away with 'a crack'd heart'. The phrase can go either way, but in fact we saw that patrician make his departure with calm dignity – Coriolanus' description of him was part of an idea of his own power. Again, the play opens with the Citizens' extraordinary delusion that by killing Caius Martius they will get corn at their own price. The play ends when Aufidius' fantasy of the monstrous nature of his rival dissolves when he has killed him.

From the opening seconds of this production, the point was being also pressed that the audience have an essential part in maintaining and working through the strange powers of illusion that are being conjured up – *Coriolanus* is, thus, at one with the Late Plays in this respect. At the start, the Citizens marched down stage and addressed the audience, who have to share the notions about killing Caius Martius. At key moments throughout the play the audience is invited to consider the process of acting, and their own involvement. The full-voiced, full-bodied performance of Howard greatly helped this view of the play. He was set a problem of 'acting', and we were to know it. Coriolanus is all voice, needing voices to keep him alive, his body craving 'voices' in the public world of the city. Here was Howard's enormous power, and intelligence. His range of voice is in any case extraordinary, and as Coriolanus he could speak a whole battery indeed of voiced parts. The man's domination on stage is done by voices – if Coriolanus is not overcoming, if he is not 'with every motion . . . tim'd with dying cries', not making an audience yield utterly, even at great cost to himself, then he is lost. When the crowd start doing their own insisting, chanting 'It shall be so, it shall be so', then he vanishes. 'Rome', the name of the stage-locations, wakes up to find that he has gone. He has been made to go because his 'acting' of an ideal had become intolerable in reality, as any ideal is bound to be. Then, that loss is itself intolerable. 'Rome' needs its illusions.

The end of the play is the achievement of a solution of the problem of what to do in that tragic dilemma. When Aufidius sees his dragon-lover become a human mother's son, when Coriolanus 'holds her by the hand silent', then Coriolanus must be killed. At that moment, Howard held a traditional silence, being quite deprived of voice, and becoming something else in a transformation of great power. His fabulous nature disappeared with his voice, leaving a vulnerable real man now able to touch his wife, son, mother and friend, and suggest they go in together and drink. Aufidius, astride and statue-like, attentive and still as an audience, turned his back, unable to watch his fantasy go.

Reality will not do either. The pressure throughout the play is to make the man of supreme excellence super-human: he cannot be just a family man close to tears. The play's movements are again towards hyperbole. There has been an earlier silence, held by Howard for a good twenty seconds when he was forcing himself to attend to the Tribunes, and not talk to the Citizens, just before his banishment. He had started that scene well enough, speaking like a very good, indeed impeccably good, Roman citizen, 'Th' honour'd gods / Keep Rome in safety . . .' and so on. If he could have learned there to keep a public silence, then he need not have vanished from Rome: but to do that would have been to lose his fantasy-status and become human, begin to live in a real world. He is at this point stung into colossal verbal activity by Rome's rejection of his reality on the word 'traitor', and instantly takes on fabulous stature again:

> Thou injurious tribune!
> Within thine eyes sat twenty thousand deaths,
> In thy hands clutch'd as many millions, in

Menenius (Graham Crowden), Caius Martius (Alan Howard) and Citizens in scene 1.

> Thy lying tongue both numbers, I would say
> 'Thou liest' unto thee, with a voice as free
> As I do pray the gods.

This play, in Hands' production and Howard's acting, was not at all a modern political tract on the 'class war'; it was among other things an exploration of the nature of dramatic illusion, and its uncomfortable place in society. Dictators are maintained in power by mass illusion: so are actors. Audiences need fantasies of an impossible ideal, and want to be included in the process of maintaining them. But such fantasies do not stand still, they enlarge and encroach, and when they become too much of a threat, they have to be banished; when they disappoint by turning human and into problematic reality they are called 'traitor' and killed. Either process, banishment or killing, is a loss, and that loss cannot be lived with. So as that one victim dies, having entered the stage to go to his death in a moment of blazing theatrical glory, we are asked to help to memorialise him, so that he is neither too close nor forgotten – he is enshrined in a 'tragedy', well away from the everyday, but operative in the hidden areas of the mind. In the play's last words,

> Yet he shall have a noble memory.
> Assist.

Alan Howard, described to me by many people I met on this tour as the finest actor in Europe today, brought to Coriolanus exceptional powers of physical presence, voice, intelligence, and experience. A man whose presence can be warm and witty and deeply engaging, he can also be subject to powerful rages if he feels that anything at all is in any way liable to interfere with the work of the company in presenting the very best that is possible. Touring, with its perpetual scramble to get on top of local difficulties in time, its constant moving out of any sort of familiar nest, is something very ambivalent for him, for his reception in these weeks in many European cities, after memories of *A Midsummer Night's Dream*, and *Henry 5*, was sometimes not far short of delirious. He began this tour justifiably angry about the conditions which modern economics impose on such a company, arguing passionately on behalf of the RSC backstage staff, for example that such miracles as they achieved should not have been expected as a matter of course. (I recall a Paris review of the Peter Brook/Paul Scofield RSC *King Lear* some years ago, which congratulated the British Government on so fully subsidising so magnificent an achievement, the hideous untruth of which must have caused some teeth to be ground down to the gums.) He was also, like all the company, tired. In the eighteen months since the production had opened at Stratford, he had also played, during eight of those months, almost without a night off, King Henry in the three *Parts* of *Henry 6*, Antony in Peter Brook's production of *Antony and Cleopatra*, and Rover in John O'Keeffe's *Wild Oats*. To all his parts he brings two personal qualities – very hard work in preparation, with private research about the part carried further than is common; and one-hundred-per-cent giving while on the stage.

Sitting quiet and apart one day, he developed for me a little of all his understanding of the part of Coriolanus, though he took considerable pains to make me understand that the result of all his feelings and thoughts was in the performance – 'I don't write about it. I act it.' He suggested that the man is a metaphor for Rome. Everyone has an attitude to him. They all want him to be *their* Coriolanus. Thus, the Citizens would love him if only he would *pretend* to love them, if he would manage to do his shopping in the same supermarket: Volumnia's attitude is incredible – 'were my son my husband'! Menenius lies about him, is prepared to

Caius Martius (Alan Howard), on his victorious return from the wars, greets his wife Virgilia (Jill Baker).

work away in the background politically, in order to help the Senate – they have messed things up with too many concessions, and now want to put a hard man on the streets, and Menenius has suggested that he is suitable. Virgilia is the only one who keeps her silence. For the rest, he is the battle-ground for all their problems, for the arguments between the Senators and the Citizens, between the Senators and the Tribunes, between his mother and Rome. This understanding, he said, governed the development of the singing of the word 'voices' in scene 13. 'It was an idea of Terry's. I was already emphasising the word. Terry said, 'Give it onomatopoeic resonance, take it further, make it like a street vendor.' So Coriolanus would put himself at their disposal, offer himself as part of the wheeling and dealing that his mother and Menenius have been working on, to make him Consul.' Everybody wants Coriolanus in his own image; he has to embody everyone in the play. 'Look in here,' he says, 'I have this thing inside me, this body politic. I am made up of those elements.' So when he gives up Rome, he is in a real sense giving himself up. Practically, he is rescuing Rome, but in the long term he is destroying himself. So the tragedy of Coriolanus is the tragedy of the whole play. Everyone, Howard felt, had died at the end to a great extent – 'except possibly the Citizens, who curiously have learned something, and thus have got something, possibly, out of it.' The Tribunes are finished. Menenius retires to a small cottage in Essex and grows geraniums. Aufidius struggles with his memoirs. Virgilia and Volumnia are destroyed, living together in an empty house. (Menenius and the two women, however, still have the grandchild.)

Howard was unsentimental about Menenius. Certainly he was not unlike Falstaff, but he related him to the dangerous, not-so-attractive side of that fat knight, who knew that the Prince of Wales was becoming the future King. So Menenius, with all that wit and humour, has an iron fist in his velvet glove – his description of Martius fits himself, 'a bear indeed that lives like a lamb.' Menenius admits to having lied his head off in Rome about Caius Martius. He tells the two Volscian sentries, 'Like to a bowl upon a subtle ground, / I have tumbled past the throw, and in his praise / Have almost stamped the leasing' – the 'book of his good acts' has been 'haply amplified'. Yet to Caius his bark is worse than his bite. On 'Down with that sword' he sees that Caius has a lot of the devil in him, is having a ball, – is in fact at that moment a big baby.

But for all that, Howard insisted that an aspect of Coriolanus is the sheer enjoyment he gets out of physical violence and killing. He enjoys it, and it is real. At the same time – 'all that funny stuff when he comes down from Corioles, about the poor man who used him kindly . . . and "then Aufidius was within my view / And wrath o'erwhelmed my pity." *Pity*? This is a personal thing for him, the discovery of the possibility of this in him. It is one of the first human marks in him we see. He's saying, "I'm not getting weak, am I?"' It has been said that he is tactless to greet his wife, on his return, with talk of widows and mothers that lack sons. But Howard felt that he was greeting her with what was in his mind, what he has been dealing with. 'Just as the racing-driver's wife must have in mind the possibility . . . oil and fire, glass, heat and speed: the actual thing you've been doing must be the thing that's close to you and frightening to you. It is in fact an added attraction. He doesn't pretend its a bed of roses out there. From just before the play starts, he is beginning to be something else, going out into another world, so on "mothers that lacked sons" I played it off Volumnia.'

There are so many fewer opportunities than in other tragedies for personal soliloquy, he noted: few opportunities where he expresses his own problem. This he found especially fascinating because of the use of the 'internal soliloquy' – 'in the middle of the scene he talks to himself' as at the start of scene 15 or in the market-place. It is all intensely personal, and mysterious. It is as if, he felt, through the play Coriolanus was becoming something that belonged to another world, more, even than a vampire or a superman: something more like an angel of death. He was fascinated by Coriolanus' avoidance of a mid point: 'he conceives himself in some areas to be so mother-dominated, vulnerable but by his standards so much less – babies, beggars, school-boys, virgins, eunuchs. So his notions of being something other and unearthly are tempered by these alternatives, ideas of himself kept within, largely hidden, in order to protect himself from the implications of such an angel of death.'

'There is something very macabre and Jacobean about a lot of the play. Coriolanus is so much more than a bully-boy. He is in touch with some other state or sphere, and he seems to have a complete disregard for death. Nobody in this play is killed until the end, and everyone talks about him. Nowhere in this play does somebody die. It is very weird. The war at the opening is a strange nightmare. Cominius, hardheaded and rational, finds that trying to explain this terrible thing that has started to happen blows his mind, as if almost he were describing a Dracula or a Satan. There is a whole area in the play expressing a power above the normal, growing. In that moment with his mother when she asks him to lie down he knows that it is the beginning of the end. The truth is in the things he doesn't say. He simply recognises this end, as it were of the process, the 'inevitable strokes' that it is 'fond to wail . . . As 'tis to laugh.' 'The recognition that there is Providence in the fall of the sparrow – once that is known, then . . . *pouf*. At *Holds her by the hand silent*, he is reconciled to her, takes her to him, makes it happen, but now a line or two later, on "But let it come" he belongs elsewhere.' He pointed out the Shakespearean three words, 'Ripeness is all', 'The readiness is all', 'let it come' with which tragedy moves into another realm; the hero is beyond moral consideration, and moving up into the empyrean: he quoted Christ's, 'Let this cup pass' in Gethsemane.

The play can be so precise, but only Coriolanus seems to know his way round this pervading mystery of 'elsewhere'. In early days of rehearsal, apparently, a good deal of time was spent calculating how far Antium was from Rome, how long was that exile for which he wanted a kiss of equal length. Howard, now, was convinced that the 'world elsewhere' was the 'city of kites and crows'. 'He goes into the desert – a natural reminiscence, possibly, of meeting Satan as Christ did. Everywhere he goes it's scorched earth, salt, ruined buildings, kites and crows picking off dead bodies. He says, "I did this".' He saw that growing element in the play as connected with the uncompromising nature of the man. 'He is always Rome's ultimate deterrent. He always beats the Volscians, always. Now, think what it would have done in 1945 to call an Atom-bomb hero "Mr Hiroshima". What a terrible thing that would be to be branded with the name of the city you have destroyed, and for ever after condemned. Worse, society would think in terms of trying to normalise him by giving standard rewards. A warrior, poet, mathematician, scientist, saint, martyr, any individual that becomes one of those things but is not satisfied is like Isaac Newton saying he had found "a smoother pebble or a prettier shell than ordinary, while the great ocean of truth lay all undiscovered before me". Though society says, "You've done it" he has to reply, "I've only just started, I haven't done anything." Society is not interested in that, and is faced with the terrible problem of what to do with the hero who won't take any reward. The normal method of controlling is the Upper Chamber, the Civil List. Supposing that then he – Mr Hiroshima – won't lie down – the world gets worried. That uncompromising state will not do. Here is a candidate for a mental home – or a cross. There is a lot of that in that man under the imagery.'

'The Devil, an Angel of Death made for death, a dragon or a god – where is he between that and "gracious silence, hail"? He doesn't want to get involved in all the rabitting and the chat and the politics: he knows it as a stupid thing – "Don't make me wear that stupid garment" he says. His tiny encounter with First Citizen in that scene ("The price is, to ask it kindly") is a sudden understanding between two rude people for a moment: he is sure of himself. Caius Martius just can't lie. He is one of the few heroes who simply cannot act – quite unlike Hal or Henry 5 or Hamlet.'

Approaching the end, Howard found something very strange about being a beggar-man to go muffled to your worst enemy. Coriolanus, he felt, is by then weary of it all, and he is pretty confident that Aufidius will finish him – not there and then, but sooner or later. His impact on Aufidius' household is equally odd. In scene 12, a Volscian had described him as 'the devil', to which Aufidius had retorted 'Bolder, though not so subtle'. Now in scene 23 there is talk of 'witchcraft' in him, and the Volscian soldiers use him as 'the grace 'fore meat'. Yet Coriolanus' choice has been right, to go to the mirror of the Roman world. Aufidius is not of course a noble savage, but a hugely subtle and highly proficient politician, whose warrior-qualities are on the wane (a stage incidentally that Coriolanus quite avoids. He is not prepared to compromise his warrior-caste). Aufidius is not winning. Howard said, 'He needs to renew himself, and so – a very primitive thing – will "renew me in his death". By killing Coriolanus he will take on his powers. When they shake hands it is a diabolical moment. Coriolanus knows that in that agreement he will go to his death – but it will be worse for Aufidius. The deal that is done – "stand by me in this cause" – means that the ultimate moment is going to happen. Between two Samurai, honour has been compromised. The way that Coriolanus makes it happen at the end throws Aufidius. Coriolanus ensures that it gets out of hand. The clean stroke is all right, but the treading to death looks ghastly. Coriolanus cries, "Come on, all do it, all do it", and the speech heading on "Kill, kill, kill, kill, kill" is *"all Con"*. Aufidius of course *has* lied, he has not writ his annals true. Does he perhaps go mad trying to write his history, afterwards?'

Howard said that he used to think the ending of the play, as a comment on love, very pessimistic, as if it were saying that there cannot be pure love, that love does ask for compromise, negotiation, obligations. Coriolanus' mother is trying to pull him, and it seems he dies for those sorts of reason, and Howard found it depressing. Then he realised that Coriolanus dies in a kind of exhilaration, as a creature from a different sphere: as if he had been someone far beyond even the superman, and he has to go back to the strange people he came from. His trip has ended, and he has to return – perhaps to Mars? – leaving the mayhem behind that the others have created. No father is ever mentioned – it is as if his mother bore him alone, almost like the virgin birth of a god: and Coriolanus is attended by three women everywhere, making a sort of *pietà*.

It is, Howard reiterated, a very dense play indeed. He was disturbed lest anyone should think that in a few hours of talk we had done any sort of justice to the play, or to his thoughts and feelings about it. 'What Terry did sublimely well was to make the play available, make the hundreds of options clear, allow the shift and varieties of opinion in the play to come through.' From the earliest days of working on it, they had all been aware of the movements inside the play, which seemed to be of two kinds. An event happened, or something was said, which coming a moment earlier or a moment later would have fixed a direction, but as it was, it just did not do it.

Similarly, they all found that they would find a firm position to talk about a matter, which would then hold for only about twenty lines. 'The play has been done such a disservice in the past: people have approached it with a mind made up, which is wrong, even though it is invitingly full of concrete images – "stone walls", "one nail"' – which describe a fixed world as well – that world of T. S. Eliot's poem.'

'There is something of Coriolanus in every single person: a romantic desire to get on with what I want to do, making possibilities against a gathering bureaucracy, a human instinct for emphasis on the individual's rights, yet still within a society. This is something deeply in the Christian mythology. It would be very interesting to see what would happen if *Coriolanus* were to be played in a Buddhist society.'

He now found the end equally disconcerting, in that the play was thrown into the laps of the audience, asking 'What are you going to do about it?' 'It is not the ending of *Hamlet*. It is more the world of Earl Mountbatten's funeral: we are all asked to assist. Everyone has been guilty and not guilty; everyone acting for the right reasons and for the wrong reasons. The people who go wrong in the play, who make the tragedy, are not aware of events perpetually moving: too many people are in a position of stone. What's bleak is that you can't absolutely point the finger at anyone else. *We* are never let off the hook: everyone in the firing squad has live bullets. Talking to people afterwards, some of the audience, actors, friends, I found that they were left in a very peculiar state of extremes of exhilaration and exhaustion, unhappy and hopeful, emotions heavily engaged, trying to work out what was right or wrong.'

The 'Coriolanus' company on tour

Maxine Audley, *Volumnia*
Jill Baker, *Virgilia*
Paul Basson, *Young Martius*
Derek Brain ('Jake'), Electrician
Bernard Brown, *Cominius*
Bille Brown, *Second Volscian Citizen*
John Burgess, *Sicinius Velutus*
Peter Cameron, trumpet
Lucy Coghlan, Make-up and Wigs
Pat Connell, *Aedile*
Ron Cook, *Sixth Roman Citizen*
Graham Crowden, *Menenius Agrippa* (Paris to Hamburg)
Charles Dance, *Tullus Aufidius*; *Caius Martius Coriolanus* 7 and 8 April
Richard Derrington, *Fourth Roman Citizen*
Philip Dunbar, *Second Roman Citizen*
David Fairclough, Assistant to the Tour Manager (Amsterdam to Zürich)
Tina Faulkner, Assistant to the Tour Manager (Vienna)
Oliver Ford-Davies, *Junius Brutus*
Nigel Garvey, timpani
Cynthia Gilman, Wardrobe Assistant
Mike Hall, *Second Roman Senator* (Paris to Hamburg); *First Roman Senator*, *Nicanor*
         (Hamburg to Zürich)
Terry Hands, Director
Brian Harris ('Basher'), Electrician
Roger Harrison, percussion (Paris, Vienna)
David Hissey, trombone
Philip Hoare, Stage Manager
David Hobbs, *First Volscian Citizen*
Duncan Hollowood, horn
Sue Honey, Wardrobe Mistress
Alan Howard, *Caius Martius, later Coriolanus*
Caroline Howard, Assistant Stage Manager

Stephen Humphries, *Young Martius*
Paul Imbusch, *First Roman Senator, Nicanor* (Paris to Hamburg); *Menenius Agrippa*
        (Hamburg to Zürich)
Stephen Jenn, *Second Volscian Senator*
Ian Judge, Assistant Director
Gordon Kember, Music Director
Christopher Lacy, flute
Ken McClellan, *Second Roman Senator* (from Hamburg)
Tony McVey, percussion (Amsterdam to Zürich)
Alistair Minnigan, Chief Stage Technician
Iain Mitchell, *Seventh Roman Citizen: Tullus Aufidius* 7 and 8 April
John Moore, Sound Technician
Deirdra Morris, *Gentlewoman*
Brian Newman, horn
John O'Mahoney, Property Master
Maureen Proud, Assistant to the Tour Manager (Paris)
Roy Purcell, *Titus Lartius*
Nigel Roberts, oboe/cor anglais (Amsterdam to Zürich)
Neil Robson, Chief Stage Technician
Hal Rogers, Tour Manager
Ruth Rosen, *Valeria*
Barrie Rutter, *First Roman Citizen*
David Shaw-Parker, *Fifth Roman Citizen* and *Third Volscian Citizen*
Garry Spraggett, Electrician
Desmond Stokes, *First Volscian Senator*
Andrew Swinnerton, oboe/cor anglais (Paris, Vienna)
Mike Taylor, Electrician (Paris, Vienna)
Roderick Tearle, trumpet
Peter Tullo, *Volscian Lieutenant*
Diane West, Deputy Stage Manager
Sue Whitmarsh, Tutor and Chaperone
Peter Whittaker, bassoon
Arthur Whybrow, *Third Roman Citizen*
Bill Wilkinson, Financial Controller, Royal Shakespeare Theatre

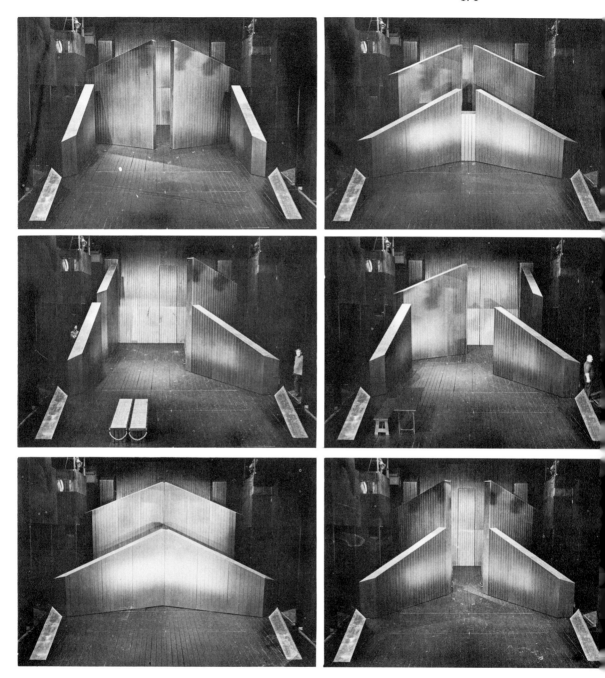

Some of the many positions of the set.

Illustration
Acknowledgements

Reg Wilson
Pages 2, 7, 22, 23, 24, 27, 28, 29, 31, 32, 33, 36, 37, 39, 41, 42, 43, 75, 82, 95, 99 (right), 108, 109, 111, 147, 151, 157, 159, 161, 163.

Royal Shakespeare Company
Pages 3, 12, 13, 16, 30, 130, 171.

David Daniell
Pages 6, 9, 10, 46, 48, 57, 67, 72, 77, 85, 97, 106, 114, 133, 136.

Reinhard Stegen
Pages 14, 50, 51, 52, 58, 79, 138, 139, 140, 141, 142, 143.

David Strong
Page 17.

Joe Cocks Studio
Page 18.

Army Public Relations
Pages 54, 99 (left), 112, 113, 115, 116.

Fayer, Vienna
Page 66.

Thalia-Theater/Meyer-Veden
Pages 90, 91.

Vera Tenschert
Pages 118, 119, 121, 123, 124.